Office of Arts and Libraries

Library Information Series No. 18

Keys to Success:
Performance Indicators for Public Libraries

**A manual of performance measures and indicators
developed by King Research Ltd**

London: HMSO

ISBN 0 11 430048 8

Contents

Preface   **v**

Foreword   **vii**

Section 1   **Introduction: why and how to use this manual**   **1**

1.1   The need to assess performance   1
1.2   Levels at which performance assessment is conducted   2
1.3   What is performance and how can it be assessed?   3
1.4   How to decide which indicator to use   6
1.5   How to derive the indicators   7
1.6   How to interpret the performance indicators   7
1.7   How this manual is set out   9

Section 2   **Performance measures used to calculate indicators**   **11**

2.1   Introduction   11
2.2   Library resources   13
2.3   Service input cost measures   17
2.4   Service output measures   18
2.5   Service effectiveness measures   20
2.6   Service domain measures   23

Section 3   **Performance indicators**   **25**

3.1   Introduction   25
3.2   Operational performance indicators   27
3.3   Effectiveness indicators   37
3.4   Cost-effectiveness indicators   49
3.5   Impact indicators   58
3.6   An example of relationships between measures   65

Section 4   **Examples of performance indicators for library services and   69
                 operational functions**

4.1   Introduction   69
4.2   Access to library facilities/premises   70
4.3   Access to library stock   71

4.4	Access to library equipment	73
4.5	Interlibrary borrowing	75
4.6	Reference and information services	77
4.7	Services to special groups	80
4.8	Activities	82
4.9	Operational functions	84

Section 5	**Methods for measuring input, output, effectiveness and domain values**	**85**
5.1	Introduction	85
5.2	Measuring staff costs	87
5.3	Measuring costs of other resources	91
5.4	Measuring service output quantities and attributes	93
5.5	Measuring service effectiveness and domain values	98

Section 6	**Methods for calculating measures and derived indicators**	**110**
6.1	Why use statistical methods?	110
6.2	Number of users and visits to the library	111
6.3	Amount of use of services in the library	116
6.4	User perception of library service attributes, user-expressed satisfaction and user-indicated importance	118
6.5	Value of public library services	123
6.6	Hand tabulations	127
6.7	Calculating derived indicators	134

Appendix A	**Understanding the methods**	**137**
A.1	Introduction	137
A.2	How to obtain input and output measures	137
A.3	Methods for obtaining measured effectiveness and domain indicators	144

Appendix B	**Glossary of terms**	**152**

Appendix C	**Performance Indicators Advisory Committee**	**156**

Preface

We in Britain are justifiably proud of our public library services, and it is evident that they are well supported by the librarians who work in them.

As part of my responsibility towards the public library service in England, I have commissioned work to create and develop management tools for our public librarians. I hope that they will be useful to both the librarians and the councillors, who, together, are responsible for the planning and managing of the public library service.

This is the second of the manuals published by my Office. It was preceded by a model costing system for public libraries. I hope that it will be followed soon by a manual on public library objectives, which I have asked the Library and Information Services Council (England) to prepare.

I am grateful to the British Library Research and Development Department for their help in managing the contracts for this work, and to the advisory committee which assisted my Office during the preparation of this manual.

It is my intention to promote awareness and use of this manual but I hope that others will share in the task and ensure that the use of appropriate performance indicators becomes an essential component of professional training.

DAVID MELLOR
Minister for the Arts

Foreword

I welcome the publication by the Office of Arts and Libraries of this manual of performance indicators for public libraries. At a time when local authorities, as part of good management practice, are increasingly turning to quantitative methods of setting and assessing performance standards, this manual should become an essential working tool for public librarians.

King Research, the team which prepared the manual, have an enormous wealth of experience in developing and evaluating performance measures of libraries and information services. They were assisted in transferring their essentially North American experience into the United Kingdom context by a small advisory committee with a breadth of knowledge and interest in the British public library service.

It is important, I feel, to approach this manual in the right way because there is a danger that the beginner could be deterred by the size of it and its depth of technical material. The first section provides a guide on how to use the manual and the contents of the various sections. Much of the scholarly and technical material which supports the main sections has been put into appendices. These are there for the more advanced user and for those who wish to establish the soundness of the main body of the manual.

It will take time for the use of performance indicators to become established and familiar practice. Already, however, some public library authorities have started the process, and it is to be hoped that the publication of this manual will encourage others to make a start. To ensure that the performance indicators manual does become an essential tool, the Office of Arts and Libraries plans to promote the development of courses and associated course material on the use of performance indicators.

ROYSTON BROWN
Chairman, Library and Information Services Council (England)

Section 1.   Introduction: why and how to use this manual

1.1 The need to assess performance

This is a challenging time for public libraries and their staff, but also a time of great opportunity. Challenging because of budgetary restrictions and the rapid pace of change. An opportunity because new techniques and technologies make us able to reach a wider community through new and enhanced services.

   This manual will help you, as a librarian, to make the most effective use of the resources available to you; in this way, you can meet the challenge and exploit the opportunities that change holds out. It is a question of reconciling the competing claims on your time and your library's money and materials.

The challenge of change

- The amount of information published doubles every 15 to 17 years. Libraries have to cope with this ever-growing volume of new publications and at the same time give their users access to about twice as much literature as they did in the early 1970s.

- At one time, libraries only had to provide access to printed materials. Today they increasingly stock information which has been captured in other ways – audio tapes, records, video recordings, computer software, microfilm and microfiche, compact and optical discs and so on. They must also make available the equipment which users need for 'reading' the information – tape recorders, record players, microfiche readers, computers etc.

- People are aware of these new information technologies, and the range and variety of information resources. They have become more sophisticated in the demands they make on public libraries and in their expectations of the information service. They are using libraries more often and more intensively.

- Many public libraries struggle to keep up with the demand for more in-depth, customised reference services. People expect libraries to open longer hours, particularly at weekends, and provide more services.

Library managers' decisions on how to allocate resources and respond to an increased demand for services and the potential for new services, all within budgetary constraints, are complex. Performance assessment helps library managers at all levels to maximise the benefits which users will gain from their public library.

How performance assessment will help you

Performance assessment will help you plan, communicate, sort out problems before they arise, make decisions, monitor progress and justify resource allocation.

Plan

Your planning will be realistic, clear and achievable because you can:

- understand what you and your library are achieving – from the points of view of managers, staff, users, community and funding body;

- set objectives and priorities for the future;

- decide how to allocate resources and predict the consequences of different allocations and different levels of resourcing.

1

Communicate	You can assess and describe your activities and: • explain how you are performing to other members of library management and staff, to the funding body and to the community you serve; • document improvements in service over time and include these in annual reports.
Sort out problems before they arise	Instead of reacting to crises you can: • identify potential problem areas – where service is deteriorating or staff are over-stretched; • understand why performance is low and take the right measures to tackle the difficulties.
Make decisions	Your decisions will take all important facts into account because you can: • gather and analyse the data you need to make each decision; • predict the outcomes of different decisions from your knowledge of how resources affect performance.
Monitor progress	You can monitor progress towards your planned goals and prioritised objectives and: • see whether you are doing the things you set out to do; • assess your future priorities for action; • achieve the most efficient performance in priority areas.
Justify resource allocation	You will inspire confidence in your funding body and back up your budget request if you: • demonstrate the relationship between the resources you are using and what you are achieving; • justify expenditure, both past and projected. By assessing performance systematically, you will be able to serve the community as well as possible and increase your own job satisfaction.
The principles of performance assessment	The gains from performance assessment are profound; its principles are simple: • Performance is the relationship between the resources that go into the library – the inputs – and what the library achieves using those resources – the outputs or outcomes. • Performance can only be measured in the light of goals and objectives – is the library doing what it set out to do? • The inputs and outputs which should be measured depend on the purpose of the assessment and the detail needed. So performance assessment is not an end in itself; but it is a means to your ends.
1.2 Levels at which performance assessment is conducted	You can assess performance on any of six levels of a library operation. The six levels are: • Resource level • Activity level • Function and service level • Location level • Entire library level.

At the *resource level* you can derive and assess the performance of the library's stock, staff, the facilities, automated system etc. Examples of resource performance are:

- productivity of staff members;

- performance of the stock – stated as the proportion of stock used over a period of time, or user satisfaction with the comprehensiveness of stock etc.

At the *activity level* you may derive and assess the performance of specific activities such as cataloguing or responding to reference enquiries. An example of activity performance is:

- cataloguing performance can be determined by the amount of cataloguing performed, the accuracy of cataloguing, the timeliness of cataloguing etc.

Performance at the *function and service levels* relates to all the activities that make up a function or service. The entire cataloguing function, for example, includes activities such as pre-cataloguing search, cataloguing, review of cataloguing etc. Thus, all the input costs of the activity must be summed and then related to the function or service output quantities and attributes.

It is also useful to consider performance at the *location level*. At this level the performance of all functions and services is assessed for the central library and each of the branches. Input costs can be determined by adding the costs of all functions and services for each location. There is no single measure of output for the functions and services in aggregate. However, the number of visits or uses serve as surrogate measures for assessment purposes. Comparisons of performance can be made across locations.

The *entire library level* involves assessment of the performance of all the locations of the library as a single entity.

1.3 What is performance and how can it be assessed?

Performance is generally considered to be the accomplishment of something. There are five aspects to performance measurement:

Aspects of performance

- What is the *object/level* of the performance measurement?

- *Inputs* — what resources are necessary to accomplish the resource, activity, service, function etc?

- *Outputs* — how much work is accomplished or how well is the activity, service, function etc accomplished?

- *Effectiveness* — how do users of the resource, activity, service etc assess its performance?

- *Impact* — how and to what extent does the resource, activity, service etc affect the community being served (that is, both users and non-users)?

Library *inputs* are the resources available and applied to support the services and products of a library. They are measured in terms of staff, facilities, stock, equipment, funding etc applied to library services. To some extent library managers have control over how these resources are allocated to the services offered by the library.

Library *outputs* are the direct results of the application of the resources. They can be measured in terms of the quantities of output produced or made available and their attributes (quality, timeliness, availability, accessibility etc).

The *effectiveness* of a library is the effect of library outputs as seen from the perspective of the users of those outputs. It can be measured in terms of user satisfaction with, and the amount of use of, library services and products. Attributes of use include purpose of use as satisfying personal needs, recreational and leisure time needs, educational needs and work-related needs.

The *impact* of public libraries is how and to what degree the community intended to be served is being served, and is partially determined by the domain they serve.

Such domains can be measured by the population or geographic area served. An important attribute of the population served is their information needs as measured by subject areas of need, types of materials needed (books, magazines, reference materials etc), and so on.

In this manual we define performance as a relationship between outputs produced, or outcomes (effectiveness or impacts), and the input resources needed to achieve those outputs or outcomes.

This manual describes a modular process for arriving at performance indicators. The primary building blocks of performance assessment are 21 performance measures (described in detail in Section 2). These 21 performance measures are organised into four groups of measures relating to service input costs, service outputs, service effectiveness and service domain (population and geographic area the library is supposed to serve). They are listed below:

service input cost measures

1. amount of resources applied to services
2. amount of money/funds applied to services
3. relevant attributes of resources applied to services

service output measures

4. quantities of output
5. quality of output
6. timeliness of output
7. availability of service
8. accessibility of service

service effectiveness measures

9. amount of use
10. user perception of attributes
11. user-expressed satisfaction
12. user-indicated importance
13. purpose of use
14. consequence of use

service domain measures

15. total population size
16. total population attributes
17. user population size
18. user population attributes
19. size of geographic area
20. geographic area attributes
21. information needs.

We have developed a conceptual framework for measuring performance which can be adapted to assess the performance of an individual, a service or a library. The framework is displayed in Figure 1.1.

Measures and indicators

Measures are indicators of size, 'goodness', use, usefulness, value etc. The measures by themselves do not convey much meaning, nor are they very useful in decision making. However, the measures can be placed into a context and relationships established between them. These relationships such as between inputs and outputs, inputs and effectiveness, effectiveness and impacts etc can be helpful to the library manager and the library's funders when assessing public library performance.

Ideally one would like to know exactly how the application of public library funds affects the quality of life, learning, work etc. This is not feasible. However, it is possible to relate the application of public library funds to the amount and quality of services provided, relate quality of services to the extent to which they are used, relate the extent of use to the purpose of use etc. In knowing these relationships public library managers and funders can approach the ideal stated above and make truly informed decisions. The relationships described above and depicted in Figure 1.1 form the basis for the performance indicators presented.

Performance indicators are derived from combinations of measures. The manual

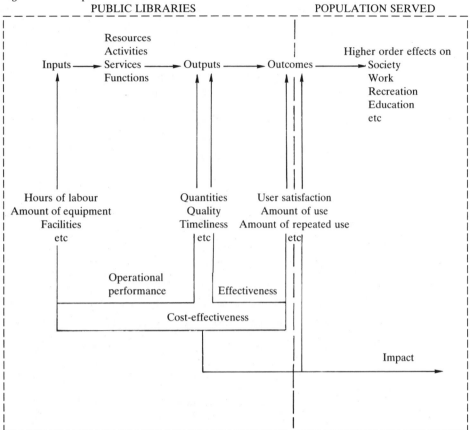

Figure 1.1 Conceptual framework

describes 16 performance indicators (see Section 3 for more details). These indicators are classified into four groups:

- Operational performance indicators

- Effectiveness indicators

- Cost-effectiveness indicators

- Impact indicators.

The *operational performance indicators* relate library input to output. Use them when making decisions about the allocation of resources to activities, services and products; the outputs to be produced (in terms of both quantities and attributes of output); the productivity of resources, activities, services and products etc.

The *effectiveness indicators* relate output to use. They represent the performance of a library, service, product etc, from the perspective of users. Use them to determine how well the user community is being served. Areas of poor performance should be investigated further and the reasons for such performance should be identified.

The *cost-effectiveness* indicators relate input to use. They are in a sense indicators of the outcome of investing resources. Note that higher level outcomes such as the consequences of using libraries can also be defined but are much more difficult to measure/derive than the cost-effectiveness indicators defined in this manual. Use the cost-effectiveness indicators in much the same way as the operational performance indicators, that is to allocate resources and decide on the desirable outcomes in terms of amount of use and user satisfaction, except that instead of considering the immediate outputs of the library, consider the outcomes of having produced the outputs.

The *impact indicators* relate the use made of the library, its services or products and the potential use that could be made of them. In other words, they are concerned with the intended service community and not just the actual users of the library and its services. These indicators represent the level of success of a library in achieving what it was set up to do. Particularly important are the reasons for non-use of the library, service or product. In a sense, the impact indicators represent the performance of the library from the perspective of its funders and community served.

The full set of 16 performance indicators and the measures from which they are derived are displayed in Table 1.1.

Table 1.1 Performance indicators and measures

Performance indicators	Measures
Operational performance indicators (relate input to output)	
Productivity	Output quantities/input costs
Cost per output	Input costs/output quantities
Cost by attribute levels	Average input costs by levels of output attributes
Productivity by attribute levels	Productivity by levels of output attributes
Effectiveness indicators (relate output to use)	
User satisfaction	Satisfaction rating scores/number of ratings
Turnover rate	Amount of use/output quantities
Amount of use by attribute levels	Average amount of use by levels of output attributes
Satisfaction by attribute levels	Average satisfaction by levels of output attribute
Amount of use by satisfaction levels	Average amount of use by levels of satisfaction
Cost-effectiveness indicators (relate input to use)	
Cost per use	Input costs/amount of use
Cost per user	Input costs/number of users
Cost per capita	Input costs/number in service population
Cost by satisfaction levels	Average input costs by levels of satisfaction
Impact indicators (relate use to potential use)	
Users as a proportion of population	Number of users/number in service population
Uses per capita	Amount of use/number in service population
Needs fill rate	Number of needs filled/number of needs identified

1.4 How to decide which indicator to use

The main purposes for most performance assessment are to support planning, decision-making and budget justifications. Choose indicators carefully to ensure that the effort associated with the data collection, processing and analysis is worthwhile and that a balanced conclusion is reached.

Ask yourself the following questions to assist you to select the right indicators:

- What is the purpose of the performance assessment?

- What are the problems to be solved?

- What are the specific questions that need to be answered?

- What is the level/object of the assessment (a resource, activity, service, service location, entire library)?

- Which indicators appear to be useful?

- What are the specific indicators which address the questions that need to be answered and the objects of the assessment?

Answer each of these questions carefully in the light of what you read in the last sub-section. Use data you already hold to help you. The Cipfa statistics and their associated measures are available to most public libraries and could provide a starting point. To make it easier for you to use the Cipfa statistics for performance measures, Table 1.2 displays the relationship between the Cipfa data and the 21 performance measures defined in the manual. (The relationship between the 21 performance measures and the 16 performance indicators was shown in Table 1.1.)

Table 1.2 Relationship between Cipfa actuals* and performance measures

Cipfa actuals	Performance measure(s)
1.1 Daytime population	Total population size
1.2 Resident population	Total population size
1.3 Area served	Size of geographic area
1.4 Density of resident population	Total population size
	Size of geographic area
1.5 Actual penny rate product	N/A
2.1 Normal issue period for books	Availability of service
2.2 No. allowable books on loan (adults)	Quantities of output
2.3 Overdue charges	Money/funds applied to services
2.4 Charge per requested item	Money/funds applied to services
3.1 Staff establishment	Resources applied to services
3.2 Books in stock	Resources applied to services
Books added to stock	Resources applied to services
3.3 Other materials in stock	Resources applied to services
Other materials added to stock	Resources applied to services
4.1 No. of service points open to public	Resources applied to services
4.2 Bookstock available at [date]	Resources applied to services
for immediate loan	Quantities of output
4.3 Recordings available at [date]	Resources applied to services
for immediate loan	Quantities of output
4.4 Exhibitions held during the	
year on library premises	Quantities of output
5.1 Books on loan at [date]	Quantities of output
5.2 Recordings on loan at [date]	Quantities of output
5.3 No. of terminals available for	
use by or on behalf of the public	Quantities of output
5.4 Annual issues	Amount of use
5.5 Number of requests for specific items	Amount of use
Percentage of requested books	
supplied within 30 days	Timeliness of output
Percentage of requested books	
supplied within 60 days	Timeliness of output
Total number of enquiries	Amount of use
6. Interlibrary loans issued	Amount of use
Interlibrary loans received	Amount of use
7. Paper copies supplied for users	Amount of use
Microforms supplied for users	Amount of use
Microfiche supplied for users	Amount of use
8.1 Revenue expenditure	Money/funds applied to services
8.2 Revenue income	Money/funds applied to services
8.3 Net expenditure	Money/funds applied to services
8.4 Capital payments	Money/funds applied to services

* Based on the 1985–86 actuals, excluding agency services.

1.5 How to derive the indicators

Performance cannot be measured directly. The performance indicators in this manual are all derived from various combinations of measures mentioned above (that is, input, output, effectiveness and domain).

A number of alternative methods for obtaining the measures are discussed (see Section 5) and for calculating or deriving the indicators (see Section 6). The methods that can be used for measurement associated with each of the performance indicators are displayed in Table 1.3.

1.6 How to interpret the performance indicators

Once you have determined your library's performance using one of the performance indicators, you will want to interpret the indicator value derived. This process is the assessment or evaluation of performance.

How do you know whether your library's performance as indicated by the productivity indicators is 'good,' 'average' or 'poor'? You can address this question by comparing your results internally within your own library, or externally with the performance of other libraries.

Table 1.3 Relationship between measures and methods for obtaining measures

Measures	Methods
Input costs	Resource allocation (eg staff logs)
Amount of resources applied to services	Resource allocation (eg staff logs)
Amount of funds applied to services	Resource allocation (eg staff logs)
Attributes of resources	
Output quantities	Staff records, library records, internal surveys
Output attributes	
Quality	Observation, internal surveys, peer review, expert review
Timeliness	Staff records
Availability	Library records
Accessibility	Staff records, visitor survey, general user survey, specific service survey, population survey
Amount of use	Library records, visitor survey, general user survey, specific service survey, population survey
Number of users	Library records, visitor survey, general user survey, specific service survey, population survey
User satisfaction	Visitor survey, general user survey, specific service survey, population survey
Number of persons in service population	Census records, local authority records
Number of needs	Population survey, visitor survey, general user survey, specific service survey
Number of needs filled	Population survey, visitor survey, general user survey, specific service survey

For each indicator we give guidance on the most appropriate ways to make comparisons. Here we need only stress that you should make sure you only compare like with like.

The most crucial – and therefore the trickiest – part of a performance assessment is deciding what actions to take. Do you wish to maintain a level of performance, to improve a level of performance or, in some instances, to lower a level of performance. In some circumstances there may be a decision to discontinue a service. Note that sometimes the performance criteria are, in effect, set by the funding body, for example by reducing budgets, deciding that specific services will be offered, or deciding that the library will decrease/increase its hours of service.

The decision to maintain performance needs to be carefully defined. Are the input costs to be maintained, in which case the outputs are likely to decline? Are the outputs to be maintained, in which case the input costs are likely to be increased? Or is the level of performance to be maintained, in which case the outputs probably have to be increased to keep up with the increases in input costs?

The concept of maintaining a level of performance raises a problem that many information organisations face. The consequences of adding new resources to an activity (for example, adding a staff member) on the outputs (increased or improved) can be seen clearly. The consequence of increased costs for the same level of resources (for example, increased salaries for staff) can be increased outputs (as staff become more knowledgeable and more proficient they can perform better) but only up to a certain level. After that level, productivity does not improve significantly.

A level of performance can be improved by reducing input costs while maintaining or increasing outputs, by maintaining input costs and increasing outputs (producing more or better or faster etc) or by increasing outputs more than increasing input costs.

For each indicator, we also list the factors which can be varied to improve performance.

1.7 How this manual is set out

Section 2 describes the five basic resources associated with public library services. These resources are:

(1) finance
(2) staff
(3) facilities and premises
(4) equipment and systems
(5) stock.

We look at how to measure these resources:

- attributes – competence, age, ownership etc;

- monetary cost – purchase price, maintenance costs, salaries etc;

- amount – how much, how many or how large they are.

Section 2 then describes 21 performance measures from which you can derive all library performance indicators. The measures are of four types:

(1) SERVICE INPUT COST MEASURES
These allow you to measure how much it is costing you to deliver a given level of service.

(2) SERVICE OUTPUT MEASURES
These allow you to measure the outputs of your service.

(3) SERVICE EFFECTIVENESS MEASURES
These are ways of measuring how effective the outputs of your library are from the perspective of your users.

(4) SERVICE DOMAIN MEASURES
These are ways of measuring the size and characteristics of the area and the population that the library serves. How many people does the library serve? What are their information needs, and how many of them are actually using the service?

In **Section 3** you will find 16 performance indicators for public libraries. We derive all of these from the 21 performance measures of Section 2. Performance indicators also fall into four classes:

(1) OPERATIONAL PERFORMANCE INDICATORS
These indicate the relationship between the outputs of your service and the resources you need to produce them.

(2) EFFECTIVENESS INDICATORS
These indicate how much people are using the service and how satisfied they are with various aspects of the service.

(3) COST-EFFECTIVENESS INDICATORS
These indicate how much your service is costing for each use, each user and each potential user.

(4) IMPACT INDICATORS
What proportion of the people who could use the service are using it? How often do people use it and how often do they find exactly what they need?

For each performance indicator we examine:

- the measures from which it is derived

- the methods used to obtain the measures

- whether an increase in the value of the indicator shows that service has improved or deteriorated

- related indicators

- examples of how to apply the indicators.

We then consider how these indicators can usefully be compared and suggest how to set about improving performance on the indicators.

Section 4 of the manual presents performance indicators for each of seven services provided directly to the public and an example of an operational function. The services are:

- access to library facilities/premises

- access to library stock

- access to library equipment

- interlibrary lending

- reference and information services

- services to special groups

- activities

- acquisitions (as an example of an operational function).

Section 5 describes methods for measuring input costs, output quantities and attributes, effectiveness and domain values. Particular attention is paid to input cost measures because these measures are rarely routinely kept because of the difficulty of doing so. Suggestions are made as to how costs of input resources can be allocated to appropriate services.

Output measures of quantities are more routinely maintained, but other measures such as quality and timeliness are not. Sometimes both input and output must be collected simultaneously in order to derive some useful operational performance indicators. Examples of forms that can be used to collect input costs and output quantities are provided and described in this section.

Section 5 also discusses four basic surveys that can be used to collect service effectiveness and service domain measures. Survey processes such as survey design, sample design, data collection methods, data processing and data analysis are described in substantial detail. Examples are provided of all of these processes.

Section 6 discusses methods for calculating (or deriving) the performance indicators from the various measures. Calculation procedures for estimating the service uses, the total service users, actual uses and proportions are presented step-by-step. These numeric calculations include how to make estimates of totals, averages and proportions for stratified sample surveys.

Appendix A presents concepts of cost finding, cost measures and survey methods. Concepts of statistical precision and confidence intervals are presented, along with an example and a table of standard errors of proportions that can be used to determine sample sizes when designing surveys and to determine the precision of survey results.

Appendix B is a glossary of technical terms used in the manual.

Section 2. Performance measures used to calculate indicators

2.1 Introduction

This section describes 21 performance measures.

Taken on its own, a performance measure can give a quantitative indication – of size, for example – but it does not give us an indication of performance. For example, we may know that an activity costs £2,000, but this will give us no way of assessing how well the activity is performing. However, if we know that the activity was attended by 20, 25 or 100 people we can make a meaningful assessment of performance.

By combining two performance measures in this way, we can arrive at *indicators* – whether of operational performance, effectiveness, cost effectiveness or impact. These indicators, which derive from the performance measures described in this section, form the basis for rational management decisions on services and operations.

Literally hundreds of such indicators can be derived from the 21 performance measures, and Section 3 describes some of the most useful of them. But first you should be familiar with the measures themselves.

The measures can be classified into four groups:

SERVICE INPUT COST MEASURES

1. Amount of resources applied to services
2. Amount of money/funds applied to services
3. Relevant attributes of resources applied to services

SERVICE OUTPUT MEASURES

4. Quantity of output
5. Quality of output
6. Timeliness of output
7. Availability of service
8. Accessibility of service

SERVICE EFFECTIVENESS MEASURES

9. Amount of use
10. User perception of attributes
11. User expressed satisfaction
12. User indicated importance
13. Purpose of use
14. Consequences of use

15. Total population size
16. Total population attributes
17. User population size
18. User population attributes
19. Size of geographic area
20. Geographic area attributes
21. Information needs.

Putting measures in context

Measures and indicators only mean something if they are taken in context and viewed in context.

Time

Timing is particularly important. The measures used to calculate indicators should be taken during the same time frame because the measures will vary over time (for example, costs increase with inflation, populations in areas increase or decrease, amount of use of services reflects changes in population served). The indicators that you derive from them are merely snapshots of the situation at a given moment.

A series of such snapshots will show how the situation is changing, and will furnish the information you need so that you can analyse the changes and make decisions accordingly.

Usually the measures should be taken over the same year, although some measures must be taken during the same week or month if they are to yield accurate pictures of library or service performance. This is not always easy: you may find it difficult to obtain reliable information on important measures such as the population served by the library in a given year.

Units

You must also define carefully the units being measured (for example, volumes in a collection, service transactions, users). And you must be clear about exactly what you are measuring. Are you concerned with only the main library (and not branch libraries), only online bibliographic searches, or only population over 18 years of age?

Sometimes you may be measuring only portions of services. For example, measures of amount of stock might be only for books and periodicals added during 1989. If so, all measures of input costs, output quantities, use of stock, number of users and so on must be commonly measured for books and periodicals only for 1989, and methods of collecting the data must take this into account.

The point is that the context must be clearly defined before the measures are obtained, and any presentation and/or interpretation of the measures and derived indicators should be described within the appropriate context.

Inputs and outputs

Every key measure discussed in this section affects library performance in one way or another. Some measures relate directly or indirectly to service input costs, others relate to service output quantities, while some relate to both costs and quantities. The indicators are measures of these relationships.

To measure both the cost of what goes into the service and the output of the service, you must know what resources have been used to provide services. The amount of resources used directly affects cost as well as quantity, quality and timeliness etc. Furthermore, the quality of resources also has a bearing on both input and output of services. For example, a more competent staff member may require a higher salary, but presumably will produce more and better services.

Because resources are such vital components, we shall examine their characteristics in more depth.

2.2 Library resources

Performance of public libraries depends on the availability and application of the various resources by the library. In this manual, resources are divided into five classes.

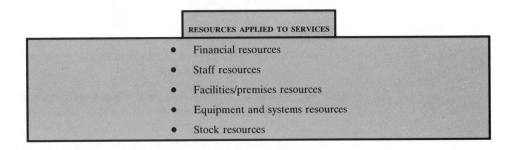

RESOURCES APPLIED TO SERVICES
• Financial resources
• Staff resources
• Facilities/premises resources
• Equipment and systems resources
• Stock resources

For a full explanation of how to measure and allocate staff costs, see Section 5.2; for measuring the costs of other resources see Section 5.3. Below, we look at each resource's attributes, costs and quantities.

Financial resources

Your library's funds include revenue and capital from local government, grants, user charges, sponsorships or income from multiple sources. In a sense, income is a measure of input of financial resource and expenditure is a measure of output.

When you actually exchange money for other resources, such as when buying supplies, paying salaries etc, you incur expenditure. In some cases it is necessary to measure the expense of the resources over time. For example, an authority may purchase property and a public library building, but spread the output of financial resources over 30 years during which the building is used. (Depreciation, expensing and expenditures are explained more fully in the glossary.)

Attributes of financial resources

- Source of funds — Possible income sources include local and central government and private donations as well as revenue generated from user charges, overdue charges etc. Where the money comes from determines both the amount of income as well as when the monies are actually received. Amounts may, in particular, vary from year to year.

- Allocation or application of funds — How a public library allocates its funds determines to a great extent both its expenditures and expenses. For example, funds allocated to capital equipment can be expensed over the lifetime of the equipment purchased. Funds allocated for staff or stock are expended during a much shorter accounting period.

- Cost of money — Interest rates are an indication of the value or cost of money.

- Inflation — Inflation erodes the level of expense or expenditure that can be achieved for a given level of income. Inflation has a greater effect on output expenditures than expenses. This is because expenses do not necessarily reflect the current value of money if they involve depreciated capital expenditures over time.

- Amount of financial resources (£).

Staff resources

Staff includes all of the people who work in or for a library. They may work full-time, part-time or in a voluntary capacity. Generally, staff input is the gross staff costs including remuneration to staff members; and the output is the total number of people on the staff, or the total hours devoted by the staff to library work.

Attributes of staff

- Level/grade of staff — Staff can be classified by level, for example, professional, clerical, manual, or by grade.

- Competence of staff — Knowledge, skills and attitudes.

- Background and experience — Education, training, years and type of experience etc.

Monetary costs of staff

- Salaries/wages — This measure (in £) should be observed over a specified period of time, such as a year.

- Gross costs — This measure is salaries or wages plus benefits and any other compensation such as bonuses. Benefits include superannuation, national insurance, car allowance etc.

- Gross costs plus overhead costs plus administration costs — There is some merit in adding other costs to the gross costs. Generally, such costs should include those that are directly identified with a staff member, including their furniture, equipment, space etc. Sometimes administration costs are allocated to staff costs as well. Administration costs include the cost of personnel, accounting and management functions, utilities etc.

Amount of staff

- Number of people on staff — The actual number of people on the staff, sometimes referred to as a head count.

- Establishment — The number of positions the library has budgeted for, including any vacant posts.

- Number of hours worked — This measure is the actual total number of hours staff have worked in the library over a specified period of time. A full year is the typical time period used because it covers a full budget cycle. For some purposes seasonal factors should be identified, so it may be important to monitor shorter periods.

- Number of full-time equivalents — This is a measure of what the total workforce would be if all staff worked full time. The hours worked by part-time employees are summed and counted as if they applied to full-time staff. Thus, a staff of 12 full-time employees and 3 half-time employees would be counted as 13.5 full-time equivalents (FTEs).

- Deployment of staff — This is a measure of how staff are actually deployed over regular and non-regular work periods (for example, evenings and Saturdays). Deployment also takes into account peaks and troughs of activity.

Facilities/premises resources

The facilities/premises of a library include all the buildings and space used for library purposes, including mobile libraries. They may be owned, rented or leased by the local authority for the library's use. The input is generally the cost of the facilities/premises, and the output is the amount of space available to the library.

Attributes of facilities/ premises

- Ownership — Whether facilities or premises are owned, leased etc.

- Central or branch library — Measures can apply to any of the library facilities/premises within an authority. Generally statistics are kept for the headquarters or main library and by branch. A third level of this attribute is mobile libraries.

- Functional areas — The space available to a library can be described in terms of the use made of various areas, for example, space allocated to technical services, open access stacks, closed access stacks, reading areas, reference and information, administration, computer room.

Monetary costs of facilities/ premises

- Cost of building — This measure includes the cost of acquiring or constructing a library building, designing it, furnishing it etc.

- Cost of building plus maintenance costs — Maintenance costs include the cost of upkeep of the building, including utilities, rent, grounds maintenance, cleaning and other maintenance services.

- Cost of building plus maintenance costs plus administration costs — This measure includes all the costs associated with the facilities/premises.

Amount of facilities/ premises

- Area — The space available to or utilised by the library or functional areas, measured in square metres.

- Number of library buildings — Number of buildings generally involves branches, although some central libraries may occupy more than one building.

- Number of mobile libraries — The number of mobile libraries available for or used by a library.

Equipment and systems resources

Public libraries use and provide access to many different types of equipment. Some equipment is used to support the library in its operation, for example, security equipment, automated systems to support acquisitions, cataloguing, issues, online public access catalogue. Other equipment is provided as a service to users, for example photocopiers.

The input is generally the monetary cost of acquiring and maintaining the equipment; and the output is measured by the number of pieces of equipment/ systems the library has available for use.

Attributes of equipment and systems

- Type of equipment/system — Equipment and systems vary from microcomputers, typewriters and terminals to binding equipment, photocopiers, printers, integrated library systems etc.

- Functional application — The various types of equipment and systems can be used to support one or more functions in the library, such as word processing, photocopying, circulation etc.

- Make, model, size, reliability, speed etc.

Monetary costs of equipment and systems

- Purchase price — The actual price paid for the equipment (through outright purchase or a hire-purchase arrangement).

- Purchase price plus maintenance costs — This measure includes the costs of maintaining or renting the equipment over a specified period of time.

- Purchase price plus maintenance costs plus administration costs — This is a measure of the total costs associated with equipment and systems in the library, including an allocation of the cost of administration.

Amount of equipment and services

- Number of pieces of equipment — The actual number of pieces/items of equipment or systems the library has.

Stock resources

Stock refers to the books, periodicals and other library materials. It can be ordered from booksellers or other suppliers, sent on approval or donated. Input is generally the monetary cost of purchasing stock, although it is recommended that other costs associated with the processing, storage and maintenance of stock be added to the purchase price to better reflect the true cost incurred. Output is measured by the number of titles or items (pieces) of stock, either in the entire stock or acquired over a specified period of time.

Attributes of stock

- Type of material — Library stock consists of various types of materials, for example, books, periodicals, sound recordings, video recordings, music scores, art works, cartographic materials.

- Subject classification — Stock may be classified into the subject categories covered.

- Age — Age or currency of the stock can be defined as the time since the material was published or the time since the library acquired it.

- Collection category — Library stock falls into various collection categories, such as adult fiction, juvenile non-fiction, reference, large-print books. Collection category also relates to open access and closed access collections.

- Publisher/source — The stock of the library can be described by the names of publishers or other sources through which the materials were acquired.

Monetary costs of stock

- Cost of stock purchases — The price paid for stock over a specified period of time.

- Cost of stock purchases plus cost of stock processing — This measure includes the cost of ordering, acquisition, cataloguing, physical processing and other activities associated with the processing of stock.

- Cost of stock purchases plus cost of processing plus cost of stock storage and maintenance — Includes the cost of shelving and storage of stock, and of binding and repairing stock as needed. Any costs associated with conservation and preservation should also be included.

- Cost of stock purchases, processing, storage, maintenance and administration — Adds on an allocation of the cost of administration.

Quantities

- Number of titles in stock — The number of unique titles in the stock.

- Number of titles purchased — The number of unique titles purchased over a specified period of time, for example the previous year.

- Number of items/pieces in stock — The number of items or pieces contained in the stock.

- Number of items/pieces purchased — This is a measure of the number of items or pieces purchased over a specified period of time, for example the previous year.

2.3 Service input cost measures

The cost of the resources that go into providing a service are the first group of key measures to consider. The resources include:

- Financial
- Staff
- Facilities and premises
- Equipment and systems
- Stock
- All other resources (for example, furniture, supplies).

There are three key types of service input costs that can be measured for each service and operational function.

SERVICE INPUT COST MEASURES
• Amount of resources applied to services
• Amount of money/funds applied to services
• Relevant attributes of resources applied to services

Amount (or number) of resources applied to services (Performance measure 1)

To provide a service, a library must apply one or more of the resources above. For example, online database searching requires reference and support staff, space for staff and service provision, terminals and peripheral equipment, reference and searching materials, photocopiers for photocopying output and so on. Generally, amounts of these resources include:

- number of staff or staff hours applied to services
- amount of space allocated to services
- number of equipment items and systems used to provide services
- communications and vendor services
- number of stock items applied or used.

Methods for determining the allocation of resources are provided in Section 5 and Appendix A.

Amount of money/funds applied to services (Performance measure 2)

A common unit of measurement for the various types of resources makes for meaningful comparisons. The amount of resources applied to services can be converted into and expressed in money terms. Once you have worked out the amount of resources applied to services, you will not find it difficult to convert these into money units using the following measures:

- wages, salaries or other compensation applied to service
- premises rent or depreciated expenditures applied to services
- equipment and system lease or depreciated expenditures applied to services
- communication charges and vendor fees applied to services
- price and cost of processing of stock items applied or used.

Attributes of resources applied to services (Performance measure 3)

You should also identify the attributes of resources because these will affect both the cost of input and the quality or quantity of output. Furthermore, specific decisions may be required regarding such attributes. For example, you may wish to measure input costs for staff. The costs will vary by level or grade of staff such as professional librarians, clerical staff, amount of experience, levels of competence or other attributes. The cost of equipment often varies with such attributes as reliability, storage capacity etc.

2.4 Service output measures

<table>
<tr><td colspan="2" align="center">SERVICE OUTPUT MEASURES</td></tr>
<tr><td>•</td><td>Quantity of output</td></tr>
<tr><td>•</td><td>Quality of output</td></tr>
<tr><td>•</td><td>Timeliness of output</td></tr>
<tr><td>•</td><td>Availability of service</td></tr>
<tr><td>•</td><td>Accessibility of service</td></tr>
</table>

**Quantities of output
(Performance measure 4)**

Here we are measuring the actual number of transactions of items provided by a service or operational function. Such quantities of service can include, for example, number of searches performed or number of items of stock provided or available, number of items photocopied etc. Examples of operational function outputs include number of items catalogued, number of items ordered and so on.

You should measure quantities of output of services for the same time period and attributes for which you measured the service input costs. And you should consider quantity of output in conjunction with other attributes of service, as outlined in the other performance measures of this service output measures group. For each output measure, keep in mind the cost and quality of resources used (Performance measures 1–3) and the quality, timeliness, availability and accessibility of the service (Performance measures 5–8).

**Quality of output
(Performance measure 5)**

Quality is an output measure which describes the grade or 'goodness' of public library services. Quality is harder to measure than timeliness, availability and accessibility and so tends to be neglected. Examples of quality measures include relevance of search outputs, accuracy of cataloguing, or level of excellence of activities. These measures must be carefully defined — sometimes quality cannot be measured directly. Quality should be measured for specific units of output, for example an item catalogued, a reference search. Usually, you should make assessments on scale values, on a scale of 1 to 5. However, you do not have to measure all transactions or units of output; instead, use sampling methods (see Sections 5.4, 5.5 and Appendix A).

**Timeliness of output
(Performance measure 6)**

Often there is a gap between the time users request something from a library service and the time they receive the output. The time gap can be measured in minutes (for example, with issues), hours or days. For some services such as online database searching, interlibrary borrowing etc, it is useful to establish a time by which users require a response. You can then measure the difference between the time the user gets it and the time by which they wanted it. For example, a user may require search results in three days to prepare a report or school assignment. If it takes four days to provide it, output is one day late. Another user may require the results in five days, so a four-day response time will more than satisfy them. Just as with quality, timeliness should be measured for specific units of output.

**Availability of service
(Performance measure 7)**

A principal measure of availability is number of hours of service, for example number of hours of service per day or per week; or number of person-hours of service, for example number of hours service is open (operating) multiplied by the number of persons providing the service during those hours. The spread of hours of availability over a week, for example morning, afternoon, evening and weekend hours, is also a measure of availability. Another example of availability is the specified loan period of materials. Availability is usually measured for a service, not a unit of service output.

Accessibility of service
(Performance measure 8)

One measure of accessibility is the distance between the service (or library) and the user. Distance can be measured in metres or miles, or in a surrogate measure such as time (for example minutes). Waiting time (for example in service queues) is an important measure of service accessibility. The time it takes users to get to a library and wait for services is a portion of the 'price' paid by users for using library services. The more users are required to 'pay' with their own time, the less likely they are to use the services.

Accessibility is a particular concern with stock, equipment etc. Stock may be inaccessible if kept in remote storage or compact storage. Public access terminals may be inaccessible if they are used a great deal. Distance is observed for the entire library or for specific services by individual users. Waiting time involves specific service transactions, whereas remote storage, for instance, involves certain items of stock or equipment.

Finally, accessibility is an important consideration for people with disabilities. Physical accessibility can be assessed in terms of the existence of facilities such as wheelchair ramps and parking spaces, or by rating the degree of accessibility using scales (1 to 5). Psychological barriers to using a library can also create accessibility problems: if the population served perceives the library or service as inaccessible, they will use it less. Perceptions of accessibility to the library and its services on the part of the population served will have an effect on the amount of use that is made of them.

2.5 Service effectiveness measures

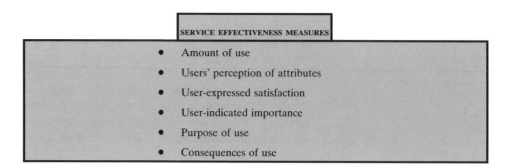

SERVICE EFFECTIVENESS MEASURES

- Amount of use
- Users' perception of attributes
- User-expressed satisfaction
- User-indicated importance
- Purpose of use
- Consequences of use

Amount of use (Performance measure 9)

The more a library or its services are used, the more effective it is. The amount of use of a library can be measured by the number of visits to it – although there are other uses as well, such as telephone calls to the reference service.

Service use can be measured in several ways. Stock use can be the number of items loaned or amount of reading.* Uses of services should clearly define and specify what is meant by use, such as requests for reference service, or number of items issued, use of photocopying equipment, that is, an occasion of use, an article or a page photocopied. For some services, the amount of use is the same as the amount of service output. These amounts are demand-driven. That is, the amounts are largely determined by users, and the extent to which users will use these services depends a great deal on output and service attributes such as quality, timeliness, availability and accessibility. On the other hand, the amount of use of some services such as access to stock does not correspond to output quantities, for example number of items of stock.

Just as with service outputs, each service and unit of use has associated attributes that are related to the extent of use. These attributes that are related to the extent of use include users' perceptions of service performance, the levels of satisfaction they express with services, their indication of how important the services are to them, the purposes for which services are used and consequences of use. These attributes are very relevant to the use, usefulness and value of public libraries, and are, therefore, considered key measures.

Users' perception of attributes (Performance measure 10)

Perceptions of services and service attributes can be measured by asking users to rate services and attributes (see Section 6 and Appendix A for discussions of the strengths and weaknesses of rating, ranking and other measurement approaches). Service ratings can be measured in general.

For example, a general service performance rating of reference services could be:

Very bad	Bad	Neither good nor bad	Good	Very good
1	2	3	4	5

Specific attributes such as relevance of response might be:

Not at all relevant	Slightly relevant	Relevant	Very relevant	Extremely relevant
1	2	3	4	5

*Book reading can be defined as a single incidence of reading (that is, an occasion in which the book is picked up and read) or the sum of occasions of reading during a loan (or some other) period. For reading of public library materials, the latter definition is suggested (although if two people read the book, perhaps two readings should be counted).

Some service attributes are readily observable and so users' perceptions of these do not always have to be measured. For example, response time should be known by both the library and the user and, therefore, can be recorded at the library and/or reported by users (on a survey questionnaire).

User-expressed satisfaction (Performance measure 11)

How well a public library service satisfies information and service requirements determines to a large degree how extensively users will continue to use them. It is difficult for users to describe their satisfaction with how well services meet their information needs and service requirements, but they can quite easily rate their satisfaction on numeric scales. For example, users can rate their satisfaction with timeliness of response of a reference search as follows:

Very dissatisfied	Dissatisfied	Neither satisfied nor dissatisfied	Satisfied	Very satisfied
1	2	3	4	5

Satisfaction probably should be measured in the context of either specific needs or specific requirements. For example, one should measure satisfaction with reference response time and/or with relevance of response.

User-indicated importance (Performance measure 12)

Another measure related to satisfaction is the importance of information needs or requirements or of attributes of a service. If users are very satisfied with an aspect of service which they do not consider important, this has different implications for frequency of use from the case where they are very satisfied with a service which they consider very important. Importance can (and should) also be measured for services in general and for specific attributes of services. Importance can also be measured with rating scales. Thus, importance of photocopying services could be rated:

Very unimportant	Unimportant	Neither important nor unimportant	Important	Very important
1	2	3	4	5

One could rate importance of levels of availability such as loan period thus:

Importance of having loan period more than	Very unimportant	Unimportant	Neither important nor unimportant	Important	Very important
One week	1	2	3	4	5
Two weeks	1	2	3	4	5
Three weeks	1	2	3	4	5
Four weeks	1	2	3	4	5

If interested in comparing across library services one can ask users to rank services in order of their importance.

Purpose of use (Performance measure 13)

Public library stock and services are used for many purposes, each of which affects the value derived from the use of public libraries. One relevant way to categorise purpose of use is as follows:

- Personal needs — Including coping with day-to-day problems, keeping informed, dealing with life's traumas etc.

- Recreational and leisure-time needs — Includes novels, hobbies, activities etc.

- Cultural needs — Includes art, literature, cultural exchange etc.

- Educational needs — Includes career change, personal development etc.

- Work-related needs — Includes professional reading, reference information etc.

Consequences of use
(Performance measure 14)

All of the purposes of use have some implications for the quality of life, the economy and other higher order effects. Even though we cannot easily place values on such consequences of use, it is useful to consider them and how use of library services affects them. At least statements of consequences can be made.

2.6 Service domain measures

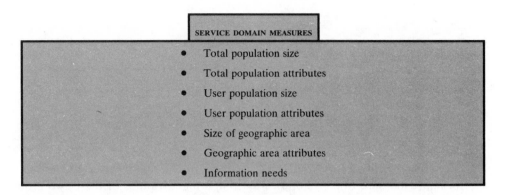

SERVICE DOMAIN MEASURES
• Total population size
• Total population attributes
• User population size
• User population attributes
• Size of geographic area
• Geographic area attributes
• Information needs

A public library's domain is its sphere of influence in terms of the population and geographic area served and the information needs of the population served. Domain measures of population and area include their size and attributes. Information needs concern informative content needed for the purposes of use mentioned above, such as information about local transport to cope with day-to-day problems, information about hobbies such as cabinet making, information about Asian countries for cultural exchange, and information about a new tax law for work-related needs. Such information needs are measured by the frequency with which such needs occur within the population and area served by the public library. There are seven domain measures discussed below.

Total population size (Performance measure 15)

This is the total population which the library is supposed to serve, whether or not it actually uses it. Population can be segmented into groups with common characteristics that may affect the use of public libraries. It is well known, for example, that people with higher levels of formal education use public libraries more often than those with less education, and registered borrowers visit libraries more frequently than others. Segmentation can be used to explain user behaviour, and decisions about running library services can be influenced by indicators related to population segments.

Total population attributes (Performance measure 16)

A distinction is made between the entire population served by public libraries and that portion which actually uses the libraries. The distinction is useful because it allows us to determine the proportion of the population served and to examine why non-users do not use the library, for example because they are not aware of it, feel negative towards libraries, lack education.

Population attributes of particular interest to public libraries include:

- residents within authorities' boundaries

- day-time population within authorities' boundaries

- catchment population determined by functional neighbourhood population attractors as measured by planning departments.

Other meaningful population or demographic attributes include categories of:

- age

- sex

- education

- occupation

- disadvantages

- disabilities

- background.

Population behaviour also depends on awareness of the library and its services as well as general attitudes concerning specific public libraries. Thus, these two population attributes should be measured from time-to-time.

User population size
(Performance measure 17)

The user population size can be measured in several ways:

- registered borrowers (current or otherwise)
- visitors
- users (of specific services).

User population attributes
(Performance measure 18)

We can learn a great deal about those who use and those who do not use public libraries by comparing attributes of these two groups. Sometimes public libraries are specifically required to serve certain segments of the population such as pre-school children, young adults, people with literacy problems and so on. The same attributes as were described for the total population above are important even so.

Size of geographic area
(Performance measure 19)

Public library performance is affected to some degree by the size of the geographic area served. In particular, large areas typically have lower use per capita and outreach programmes are more costly. The principal measure of geographic area is hectares.

Geographic area attributes
(Performance measure 20)

Attributes related to geographic area which are of interest to public libraries are:

- population density
- degree of urbanisation
- transport type and availability
- existence of physical barriers to travel to public libraries such as roads, rivers, hills etc.

In addition to the size of a geographic area, the attributes above can also have a bearing on public library use and, therefore, performance.

Information needs
(Performance measure 21)

Information needs are, in a sense, attributes of the population. Needs can be measured by the number of people who need certain types of information (for example described in terms of subject matter) and for types of information materials (for example fiction, non-fiction, large print, audio-visuals). Since each individual has more than one kind of information need and multiple instances of the same kind of need, the total information has to reflect the totality of needs across the entire population served.

Information can be measured by observing critical incidence of need and how the needs were met, for example from a library, a friend, a professional (doctor, solicitor, accountant etc), newspaper, magazine and so on. We can then go one step further and establish the consequences of satisfying the need (Performance measure 14) such as saving time or money in travel or shopping, making a better cabinet, getting well faster etc.

Section 3. Performance indicators

3.1 Introduction

In Section 1 performance was defined as a series of relationships between:

- resources available to a library
- outputs produced by a library
- use of the library.

Performance then is about relationships rather than absolute measures. In further developing this concept of performance as a relationship between measures rather than as absolute measures, the following classes of indicators can be identified:

- operational performance indicators
- effectiveness indicators
- cost-effectiveness indicators
- impact indicators.

The *operational performance indicators* relate input to output. Use them to make decisions about:

- how you allocate resources to activities, services and products;
- what outputs you intend to produce (both the quantities and attributes of outputs);
- how productive are resources, activities, services and products etc, or how productive should they be?

The *effectiveness indicators* relate library or service output to use. They indicate how well your library, service, product etc is performing in the eyes of users. Use them to determine how well the user community is being served. Investigate further areas of poor performance and uncover the reasons behind them.

The *cost-effectiveness indicators* relate input to use. They are in a sense indicators of the return on investing resources. Thus, public library funders are particularly interested in cost-effectiveness indicators. Note that higher level outcomes such as the consequences of using libraries can also be defined but are much more difficult to measure/derive than the cost-effectiveness indicators in this manual. Use the cost-effectiveness indicators in much the same way as the operational performance indicators, that is to allocate resources and decide on the outcome you wish to achieve – amount of use and user satisfaction; only instead of considering the immediate outputs of the library, consider the outcomes of having produced the outputs.

The *impact indicators* relate the use made of the library, its services or products to the potential use that could be made of them. These indicators represent the level of success of a library in achieving what it was set up to do. Particularly important are the reasons why the library, service or product is not used. In a sense, the impact indicators represent the performance of the library from the perspective of its funders and the community it serves.

In this section each class of indicator is described. A total of 16 performance indicators have been identified as follows:

OPERATIONAL PERFORMANCE INDICATORS

1. Productivity
2. Cost per output
3. Cost by attribute levels
4. Productivity by attribute levels

EFFECTIVENESS INDICATORS

5. Turnover rate
6. Amount of use by attribute levels
7. User satisfaction
8. User satisfaction by attribute levels
9. Amount of use by satisfaction levels

COST-EFFECTIVENESS INDICATORS

10. Cost per use
11. Cost per user
12. Cost per capita
13. Cost by satisfaction levels

IMPACT INDICATORS

14. Users as a proportion of population
15. Use per capita
16. Needs fill rate.

When applied to a particular library service or product, activity etc, specific versions of these 16 performance indicators can be used according to the performance assessment wanted. As an example, consider the cost-effectiveness indicator Cost per use. This could be applied as total cost per issue, staff hours per reference enquiry filled, cost per interlibrary loan etc. Section 4 includes detailed lists of indicators for various library services and operational functions.

The descriptions of each of the 16 performance indicators include:

- the measures used to derive the indicators (see also Section 2 for details of the measures);

- the measurement methods that can be used (see also Section 5 for details on measurement methods and Section 6 for how to calculate or derive indicators);

- related indicators and specific examples of each indicator. The nature of the correlation, which relates the value of the indicator with performance, is included. A positive correlation implies that the higher the value of the indicator the better the performance of the library. A negative correlation means that the higher the value of the indicator the worse the performance.

We also discuss how each performance indicator can be used. First, we consider internal (within library) comparison or analyses. Then we discuss possible external (library-to-library) comparisons or analyses. Finally, we suggest some actions that can improve performance on the indicator.

3.2 Operational performance indicators

Operational performance indicators express the relationship between the outputs your library produces and the input resources needed to produce these levels of output. For example:

- For an operational service, the cost per reference transaction is an indicator of the performance of the reference service. *This is an average or unit cost indicator*;

- For an operational function, the number of books catalogued per staff hour is an indicator of the performance of the cataloguing staff. *This is a productivity indicator*.

These two types of operational performance indicators are the inverse of one another: a rise in unit costs indicates a drop in performance; a rise in productivity indicates a rise in performance. Each type of measure, then, has its own special meaning and uses.

As discussed in Section 2, the input costs are not necessarily the monetary costs to provide a service or product. They represent the application of resources needed to provide a service or product. Similarly, the outputs produced refer not only to the quantities produced, but also to the various attributes of the output, for example, quality, timeliness, availability, accessibility.

The operational performance indicators in this section give us an idea of what our library can expect to achieve with a given set of resources; or, conversely, what resource will be needed to produce certain quantities of output with particular levels of quality, timeliness and so on.

For example, comparisons of the productivity of staff members performing the same activities can help to identify staff who perform especially well or especially poorly. They can also be used to develop productivity objectives. Note that the development of productivity objectives should be negotiated between the staff actually performing the activities for which the objectives are being set and the supervisors/managers of those activities.

Four operational performance indicators have been defined (see Section 2 and the Glossary for definitions of attributes):

Operational performance indicators
• Productivity
• Cost per output
• Cost per attribute level
• Productivity per attribute level

Productivity is the direct relationship between the quantities of output of a process or service and the resources used to produce that output. The input resources are usually measured in terms of the monetary costs or the hours of staff time associated with the production of the outputs. Productivity indicators are, in a sense, indicators of the return on investment in library resources.

Productivity indicators gives an idea of how much can be produced from a given set of input resources. An example is the number of items that can be catalogued per hour spent by staff. You can use this information to decide on the amounts of resources that are needed to produce additional output.

Figure 3.1

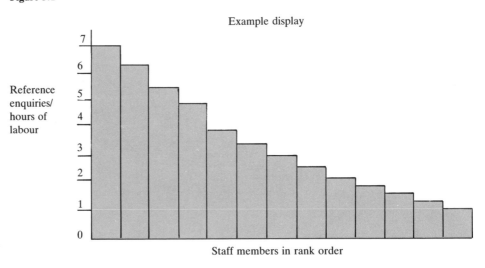

In this example (Figure 3.1), productivity of several members of the reference staff is displayed. The display ranks productivity from the most to the least productive staff member. In this situation a library manager probably would look into why some staff have particularly low productivity or why there is such a difference in productivity. There may be a valid reason: their years of experience, level of education, the difficulty of requests assigned to them etc.

Internal comparison

As shown in the Figure 3.1, staff productivity can be measured for comparative purposes.

One can also observe the productivity of individual staff over time for their annual staff reports and for decisions on pay rises or promotions. However, for some services quality and timeliness of services must also be taken into account.

The productivity of a resource, activity or service etc can be compared over time to monitor change, especially if the input costs have changed. Suppose that input costs are increasing steadily over time. The indicator can predict how much output quantities will fall unless other changes (to the resources allocated or the procedures, policies etc) are implemented.

Across services

The productivity of an activity or service can also be compared with the productivity of other services to see which are achieving the greatest return on investment. You should not discontinue a service purely and simply because it takes a lot of resources to provide it. There may be perfectly valid reasons for high input costs or low output quantities. Nevertheless, an understanding of the productivity of each service is useful for developing budgets, allocating resources, estimating resource needs (particularly staff resources) and for developing productivity objectives.

Across service locations

A third comparison of productivity can be made across service locations for common activities or services. An example is comparing the number of reference enquiries that can be handled per hour of staff time in the various locations. Locations with lower productivity are not necessarily performing badly overall. Rather it suggests that the locations with low productivity should be investigated further.

The low productivity could be the result of more complex enquiries, the staff's inexperience with certain reference materials, or the lack of certain materials and resources. The comparison shows which areas of service need more study to determine what the problems are and what is causing them. Only then can you decide how to address the problems.

External comparison

You can compare productivity across libraries provided that you measure the same input cost elements and outputs. The comparison is useful in gauging how 'good' or 'bad' a particular productivity level is for one library relative to others.

On a service-by-service basis the cross library comparisons can help to pinpoint services which appear to perform poorly and those which appear to be doing well. This helps the library manager determine where to investigate further. But beware of drawing hasty conclusions: the productivity of a service may have been sacrificed to improve the various attributes of output. Productivity can only be interpreted meaningfully in relation to the goals and objectives set by each library.

Special considerations

In measuring productivity, it is important to define the input unit being used. Consider the number of reference enquiries handled per staff hour:

- if we use the total number of staff hours devoted to the reference service as a whole, we measure the overall productivity of the reference service;

- if we measure the number of hours devoted to dealing actively with reference enquiries, we gauge the actual productivity of reference enquiry response.

The problem is that reference is a demand-driven service. In considering the productivity of the reference service, staff are available at the reference desk regardless of whether they are serving a user or not. Consequently, the productivity of the service cannot always be improved directly. Instead:

- staff can do other jobs while waiting for the next user enquiry;

- we can allocate staff time to the reference service according to patterns of demand (for example more staff at the desk at expected peak times);

- we can increase the use made of the reference service through promotion, targeting users with special needs etc.

A similar problem exists with services like interlibrary lending. The service in general could be made more productive if the interlibrary loans were batched (see example in Section 3.6). However, if libraries wait until a batch of optimum size has accumulated, the timeliness of the service to the user could deteriorate seriously. Libraries, therefore, like all service organisations, have to decide how to trade off productivity against other attributes of output such as quality, timeliness, availability, accessibility etc.

How to improve
Productivity

- Reallocate resources
- Replace or upgrade existing resources
- Acquire new resources
- Change policies
- Change procedures
- Batch activities if possible.

PERFORMANCE INDICATOR 2: COST PER OUTPUT

Measures: Input costs/output quantities

Methods: Resource allocation, staff records, library records, internal surveys

Correlation with performance: Negative

Related indicators: Productivity, Cost by attribute levels, User satisfaction

Examples:
– Cost per item catalogued
– Cost per reference enquiry satisfied

Compare the *Cost per output* indicator across services or across libraries to see how well your library's resources are being spent.

Cost per output should be analysed in conjunction with the *Cost by attribute levels* indicator. It is these two indicators together that help determine whether and how to invest more resources to produce more and/or better outputs or, conversely, what the implications of more costly resources or reduced amounts of resources will be on the quantities (and attributes) of outputs.

This indicator is negatively correlated with performance: the lower the *Cost per output* the better the performance of your library. However, after a certain point further reductions in costs will adversely affect quality, timeliness, availability etc.

This indicator, when derived for several services offered by a library, is good to help pinpoint potential problem areas quickly. Any service with a relatively high *Cost per output* should be further investigated, particularly using the *Cost per attribute level* and *User satisfaction* indicators.

Figure 3.2

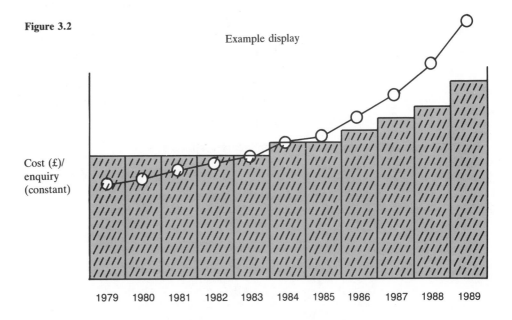

Example display

In this example (Figure 3.2), cost per unit (enquiry) is displayed over time. Also displayed is the cost per unit given in constant £, that is discounting for inflation. The cost per unit appears to reflect inflation rates until about four years ago, at which time cost per unit becomes higher than one would expect considering inflation.

31

Internal comparison	The *Cost per output* can be compared over time to monitor change, especially if the input costs have changed. If the *Cost per output* is increasing over time, the indicator can be used to predict how much it will cost to maintain or increase the numbers of outputs produced or, conversely, the likely reduction of outputs that would result from more costly or fewer resources.

The *Cost per output* is particularly useful in comparing alternative methods of providing services or performing operational functions, for example, automated *versus* manual or bought-in services *versus* in-house.

The *Cost per output* can also be compared across service locations, for example across branches for a single service. If the *Cost per output* is higher at some locations than at others, does the difference result from higher costs or lower outputs? Are there valid reasons for the differences? If not, what changes can be made to reduce the costs or increase the outputs?

The *Cost per output* can be compared across services. This gives the library manager information about the unit costs of services which, when considered together with the total costs of a service (that is the unit cost multiplied by the number of outputs), can help make decisions about which services to maintain, improve or discontinue.

Cost per output is the principal measure used to establish economies of scale of public library operations (see Appendix A for a discussion of economies of scale). Economies of scale are measured by *Cost per output* at various levels of output. You will often find that the cost of each unit of output falls as the amount of output rises – until a point is reached above which decreases are very small. This point is known as the 'critical mass' of output, and cost-wise it is the optimum level of output. Information on economies of scale can be particularly useful in determining whether certain functions or services should be performed centrally or locally in each branch to reduce the *Cost per output* (and total costs).

External comparison	*The Cost per output* is one indicator which does lend itself fairly well to comparison across libraries. However, it is important that the same cost elements are measured, the same outputs are measured and the same measurement methods are used. The comparison, when valid, can give a quick indication of how well the library is performing on various services relative to others.

If your library has a high *Cost per output* for one or more services, you may want to investigate the reasons. For example, a library in an urban area may pay higher salaries to its staff, thereby increasing its input costs. Output may be low because a library is not automated.

This indicator will help you to decide which services should be further investigated and which appear to be performing well.

How to improve *Cost per output*	<ul><li>Reallocate resources</li><li>Replace or upgrade existing resources</li><li>Acquire new resources</li><li>Change policies</li><li>Change procedures</li><li>Batch activities if possible.</li></ul>

Measures:	Average input costs by levels of output attribute
Methods:	Resource allocation, observation, internal surveys, peer review, expert review, library records, staff records, visitor survey, general user survey, specific service survey, population survey
Correlation with performance:	Negative
Related indicators:	Cost per output, User satisfaction
Examples:	– Cost by levels of cataloguing throughput time – Cost by levels of reference response quality

The *Cost by attribute levels* indicator can be used to complement the information obtained through the *Cost per output* indicator. Through them, you will recognise the relationship between the quantities of outputs and the attributes of those outputs.

Given a fixed set of resources, a library manager can decide how to balance the quantities produced, quality, timeliness, availability, accessibility etc related to a service or product. For example, with a fixed set of staff, space, equipment and other resources, the cataloguing function can produce a certain number of catalogued items in a period of time, at a certain level of quality. The trade-off here is between the quality of the cataloguing and the number of items catalogued.

The relationship between this indicator and performance is negative. It is sensible to assume that the less it is costing to produce output with a given level of attributes such as timeliness, the better the performance of the library.

Figure 3.3

Example display

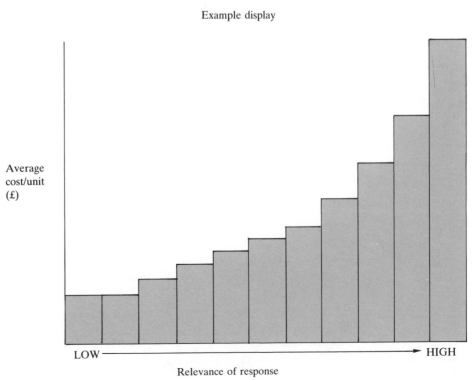

Average cost/unit (£)

LOW ⟶ HIGH

Relevance of response

In Figure 3.3 we see that it costs more (on average) to obtain higher quality (measured by relevance of response). When the relevance of responses has reached high levels, it costs a great deal to achieve further unit increase in relevance.

We could express the relationship as the ratio of average cost to average quality, or timeliness etc. Such a ratio can be used to compare alternative methods of providing services or to compare different libraries. However, by displaying the data in a bar chart, you will see at a glance how much it costs to achieve the levels of quality, timeliness, availability, accessibility and so on that you desire.

Internal comparison

There are several levels at which internal comparisons can be made:

- By comparing measures over time, we can monitor changes in the costs at each attribute level.

- The comparison can be made across the various attributes of a service or product. In this case, the comparison can be used to determine the relative costs of achieving various attribute levels. For any service, for example, is quality more costly to achieve than timeliness? If average cost falls more rapidly than timeliness deteriorates, while quality goes down, then quality can be considered more costly to the library than timeliness. Using this information, the library manager can decide which attributes of a service or product to improve or maintain.

The meaning of comparisons for a particular service, for example reference, depends on the objectives of the library and the reference service. It is most important to set priorities among the various attributes of output. Is it more important to answer enquiries very quickly or with high quality? If you have not set these priorities, measuring input costs and outputs and deriving indicators can provide the basis from which library staff will be able to set them.

- You may compare the same attribute across services. An example is the comparison of average cost per level of timeliness for reference services and interlibrary loan services. This comparison tells the library manager for which services the attributes are more costly.

- Compare across service locations for the same services. An example is the comparison of the average costs of the various attributes of reference services at the central library and branch libraries.

External comparison

The comparison of this indicator across libraries is not very useful.

How to improve *Cost by attribute levels*

- Reallocate resources
- Replace or upgrade existing resources
- Acquire new resources
- Change policies
- Change procedures.

This indicator, *Productivity by attribute levels*, relates the productivity achieved by the library to the various levels of attributes associated with the outputs produced.

For example, the number of items catalogued per hour of staff time is an indicator of the productivity of the cataloguing staff. The cataloguing productivity at different levels of quality can be derived to produce the Productivity by attribute levels indicator. This indicator tells us what the effects of achieving various levels of output attribute will be. You can decide to improve the quality of cataloguing (through one or more means, for example retrain staff, improve cataloguing, allocate more staff time) but you will be aware of any fall in productivity or rise in throughput time which is likely to result.

The relationship between *Productivity by attribute levels* and performance is a positive one. As productivity increases the performance improves.

In the example given in Figure 3.4 we assume a certain standard of quality. We then compare the productivity of staff for outputs produced above and below the standard. A variety of comparisons is made.

Staff member A has high productivity when producing at both above and below quality standards. Staff member B has somewhat lower productivity when producing above standard. Staff member C has much higher productivity when producing below standard and Staff member D has low productivity regardless of whether performing above or below standard. Each result has implications concerning remedies such as training.

Internal comparison

The *Productivity* indicator is concerned with quantitative aspects of productivity while the *Productivity by attribute levels* indicator is concerned with the qualitative and other aspects of productivity. The indicator, *Productivity by attribute levels*, can be compared for any service or product over time to monitor change.

The indicator can also be compared across staff members performing the same activities. In this way you can identify good performers and poor performers. As with the *Productivity* indicator, the *Productivity by attribute levels* indicator can be used to set performance objectives.

The indicator can also be compared for the same activities or services across service locations.

External comparison

External comparisons of this indicator are not very useful.

Figure 3.4

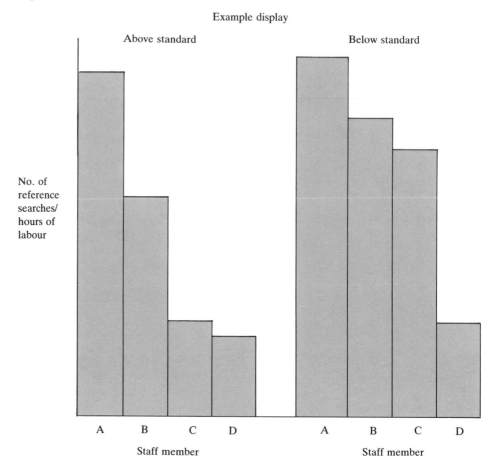

Example display

Above standard

Below standard

No. of
reference
searches/
hours of
labour

A B C D

Staff member

A B C D

Staff member

How to improve
*Productivity by attribute
levels*

- Reallocate resources
- Replace or upgrade existing resources
- Acquire new resources
- Change policies
- Batch activities if possible.

3.3 Effectiveness indicators

When we evaluate effectiveness, we view performance of a service or product from the perspective of its users. Effectiveness indicators demonstrate the relationship between what the library produces as outputs and the use that is made of those outputs. The better a library performs the greater the use of the library, and the more effective the library.

Effectiveness indicators provide information that complements the information derived from the operational performance indicators. The library manager can use the operational performance indicators to make decisions concerning the internal operation of the library. However, making these decisions completely independently of users' input could result in decisions that do not improve performance.

Five effectiveness indicators are defined in this manual:

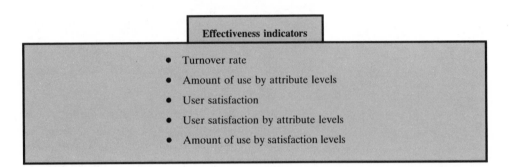

Effectiveness indicators

- Turnover rate
- Amount of use by attribute levels
- User satisfaction
- User satisfaction by attribute levels
- Amount of use by satisfaction levels

There are three possible results of using the *Turnover rate* indicator.

For demand-driven services (that is, those services which respond to user requests/demand) the number of uses will equal the output quantities.

Sometimes the quantities used equal the quantities produced but people would use a larger quantity if it could be produced. An example of this situation is the provision of service to the housebound. It is important here to attempt to estimate the potential demand/use for this service. Such information is gathered through an analysis of the service community and, together with productivity indicators for the service, can be used to predict the resources that would be needed to satisfy the potential demand.

Some services create output in anticipation of demand. These proactive services may produce more than is actually needed. An example of this is stock use. The number of items of stock in a library may exceed the number of items of stock used, and the number of uses of the stock over a period of time. Of course, care must be taken to define what is meant by 'use'. It could refer to issues, in-library uses or accesses. For example, it is important to distinguish between the:

- number of items in stock/number of items of stock used

- number of items in stock/number of uses of those items.

Number of items in stock/ number of items of stock used

This measures the overall performance of the stock itself. What proportion is used (by various means) and what proportion is not used over a period of time? Presumably one goal of any library is only to stock items which will be used while recognising that certain items of stock will be used more than others. A library that has 80 per cent of its stock used over a one-year period is performing better than a library that has 60 per cent of its stock used over the same period. But what can the lower performing library do to improve its stock performance?

The first thing is to consider which items of stock are not used and to determine why they are not used. Are they concentrated in certain subject areas that may not be relevant to library users' current needs/interests? Are they older items that have become obsolete? Are they inaccessible to the user in closed stack areas or remote storage areas? Are the library's users aware of these items? Once these questions have been addressed the library can take two sets of actions:

- *Deal with the contents of the existing stock.* Remove obsolete and unwanted items from the stock, make stock more accessible—if not physically then through finding tools such as subject guides etc, increase awareness of the stock and so on;

- *Revise stock selection and acquisition policies and procedures.* The stock development policies should be reviewed and revised as necessary to concentrate on items which are more likely to be used.

Number of items in stock/ number of uses of those items

This measures the turnover of stock. It is an indicator of how intensively the stock is used. Again, the number of uses can vary depending on which types of use are being measured.

The 'number of items in stock/number of issues' is defined as 'collection turnover rate' in the PLA Output Measures. It is more accurately defined perhaps as the 'collection turnover rate by circulation' or the 'circulation turnover rate.' The 'overall stock turnover rate' would include all types of uses: issues, in-library accesses and interlibrary loans. The rate can be greater than or less than one and is based on the assumption that the higher the turnover rate the better the performance of the stock.

Figure 3.5

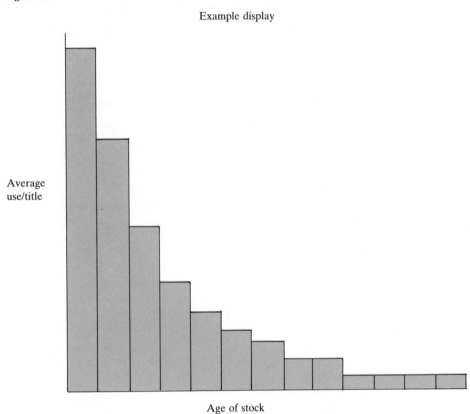

Turnover rate is the relationship between amount of use and output quantities. In the example in Figure 3.5, average use per title is displayed by age of stock, which shows that use drops dramatically over time. Such information can be used for stock management including 'weeding'.

Internal comparison

The *Turnover rate* can be compared:

- over time for a specific service or product. The effects of various actions to improve the *Turnover rate* by increasing use can be monitored over time;

- across services, for those services where the output quantities do not equal the amount of use. The comparison will provide information about the relative popularity of the services;

- across service locations for appropriate services. Again, the comparison will provide information about the relative popularity of the services at each location.

External comparison

The *Turnover rate* can be compared across libraries for appropriate services. Care must be taken to ensure that the definitions of uses and outputs are common across the libraries being compared. The comparison will provide an indication of how well a library is performing relative to others, but needs to be considered relative to the indicator *Users as a proportion of population* for a more complete picture of performance.

How to improve *Turnover rate*

- Improve attributes of service that are important to the user
- Increase awareness through promotion
- Expand or change hours of service
- Increase the number of service locations
- Expand means of access to the service
- Increase, improve or reallocate resources.

The *Amount of use by attribute levels* indicates how the attributes of output (quality, timeliness, availability, accessibility etc) affect the amount people use a service or product. An example is how use of interlibrary lending service varies with the timeliness of the service. This indicator helps us to predict how changes in attributes of the outputs of a service are likely to affect use of that service. If we also know the *Cost per use* we can work out how much it will cost to achieve the desired levels of attributes (see operational performance indicators).

The relationship of this indicator and performance is positive in that the greater the amount of use, the better the library's performance.

The example in Figure 3.6 shows that amount of use (and average use) of a service goes up if the service is available for more hours. Yet, in the example, after a certain point, increases in hours of availability do not increase amount of use very much.

Internal comparison

The *Amount of use by attribute levels* can be compared internally over time for various services. This enables us to monitor the effects of changes in attributes.

The indicator can also be compared across the various attributes of services to determine which attribute has a greater or lesser effect on amount of use. This information can be extremely useful in helping to decide which attribute of a service or product to improve. Using this indicator together with the *Cost by attribute levels* helps the library manager understand the resource implications associated with improvement of the output attributes.

The *Amount of use by attribute levels* can also be compared across service locations for each service. This will provide an indication of the relative importance of the attribute levels (in terms of their effects on use) at each location.

External comparison

A comparison of this indicator across libraries is not very useful.

How to improve *Amount of use by attribute levels*

- Improve attributes of service that are important to the user

- Identify and respond to user needs and requirements

- Develop an understanding of user expectations

- Increase awareness through promotion

- Expand or change hours of service

Figure 3.6

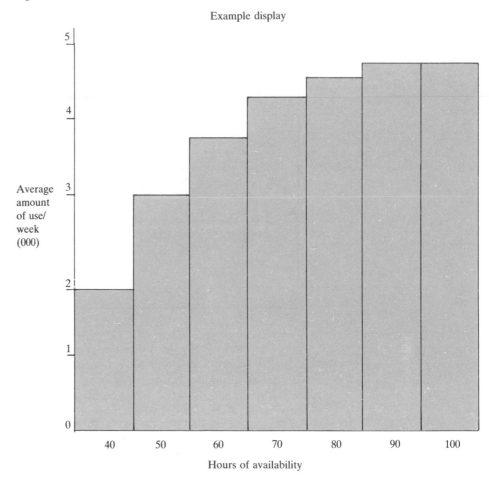

Example display

- Increase the number of service locations
- Expand means of access to the service
- Increase, improve or reallocate resources.

User satisfaction with a product or service is an indicator of performance. It can be measured at two levels:

● General *User satisfaction* with a service or product or the library as a whole.

● *User satisfaction* with specific attributes of a service or product (that is, the attributes of output).

The two levels will be measured in different ways (general question or critical incidence).

The relationship of this indicator with performance is positive in that the better a service or product is performing, the higher the satisfaction will be. Furthermore, as demonstrated later, there is a positive correlation between *User satisfaction* and amount of use. The more satisfied people are with a service, the more they use it.

Table 3.1 User satisfaction levels: Example display

Level of satisfaction	Satisfaction rating score	Proportion of users (%)
Very dissatisfied	1	(4.2)
Dissatisfied	2	(6.8)
Neither satisfied nor dissatisfied	3	(12.4)
Satisfied	4	(47.1)
Very satisfied	5	(29.5)

In Table 3.1 we display the proportion of users who express various levels of satisfaction. Such an indicator is useful to managers, particularly if it shows how many users are dissatisfied. If the number or proportion is large, we can set about establishing why they are dissatisfied. Satisfaction with outputs of individual staff can be compared using the proportions or average rating scores. The average rating of satisfaction for this example is 3.91 (see Section 6 for method of calculating average rating).

Internal comparison

The *User satisfaction* with a service or product or its attributes can be compared internally over time. We can also measure the effect of various actions taken to improve *User satisfaction* if we implement them one at a time.

43

Also, within a library, the *User satisfaction* across services can be compared and might help make decisions about which services need to be improved.

External comparison

User satisfaction with a service or product can be compared across libraries but is more difficult than an internal comparison. *User satisfaction* is a subjective measure which relates to the user's own experiences and expectations. For *User satisfaction* ratings to be truly comparable across libraries it should be normalised against a common satisfaction rating.

If a library has *User satisfaction* ratings that consistently fall in the lower quartiles relative to other libraries, then there are clear indications of problems. Those areas where satisfaction is low should be investigated in more depth, for example measuring satisfaction with specific attributes of service and determining specific reasons for low satisfaction.

Special considerations

It is important to recognise some special considerations relating to the measurement of *User satisfaction*:

- First, the more homogeneous the user group, the less the satisfaction ratings will vary. For example, a group of 20 individuals attending an activity will tend to have more similar satisfaction ratings than a group of 100 attending the same activity. This phenomenon needs to be taken into account when designing a sample.

- Second, the more focused the services the more satisfied the users tend to be. For example, the users of a small branch library tend to be more satisfied with the services than the users of a central library which offers a much greater variety of service.

- Third, new users of a service and infrequent users will tend to be more satisfied than repetitive users who are better able to discern good from bad performance.

How to improve *User satisfaction*

- Identify and respond to user needs and requirements
- Improve attributes of service that are important to the user
- Develop an understanding of user expectations
- Increase, improve or reallocate resources.

PERFORMANCE INDICATOR 8: USER SATISFACTION BY ATTRIBUTE LEVELS

Measures:	Average satisfaction by levels of output attribute
Methods:	Visitor survey, general user survey, specific service survey, population survey, observation, internal surveys, peer review, expert review, staff records, library records
Correlation with performance:	Positive
Related indicators:	Amount of use by satisfaction levels
Example:	– User satisfaction with different levels of timeliness of interlibrary lending

User satisfaction by attribute levels is an indicator of how the output of a service affects *User satisfaction*, or user tolerance for various levels of output attributes. An example is the average user satisfaction at different levels of timeliness. If timeliness is high (that is, short turnaround time) it is assumed that satisfaction will be high also. This indicator will help the library manager predict the effects of changes in output attributes of a service or product.

The relationship of this indicator with performance is positive in that the greater the average satisfaction the better the performance of the library.

Figure 3.7

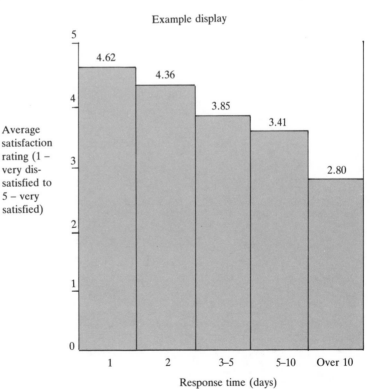

The example in Figure 3.7 shows that high response time, that is, poor timeliness, results in decreased levels of satisfaction. Library management can make decisions to improve response times (or quality, availability, accessibility etc) and know what effect such decisions will have on user satisfaction.

Internal comparison	There are several levels at which internal comparisons can be made. First, the comparison can be made across the various attributes of a service or product. This comparison can be used to determine the relative importance to the user of the various attributes. For any service, for example, is quality more important than timeliness? If average satisfaction falls more rapidly than timeliness deteriorates, while quality goes down, then quality can be considered more important to the user than timeliness. In this way we can decide which attributes of a service or product need improvement, or for which attributes performance should be optimised.
	A second internal comparison is across services for the same attribute. The comparison could be between average satisfaction per level of timeliness for reference services and interlibrary loan services. This tells us for which services the attributes are more important.
	A third comparison is across service locations for the same services. An example is the comparison of the average satisfaction with the various aspects of reference services at the central library and branch libraries.
External comparison	An external comparison using this indicator is not very useful.
How to increase *User satisfaction by attribute levels*	• Identify and respond to user expectations and needs
	• Improve attributes of service that are important to the user
	• Develop an understanding of user expectations
	• Increase, improve or reallocate resources.

The *Amount of use by satisfaction levels* relates the amount a service is used to the users' satisfaction with the service or product and its attributes. The larger this indicator the better the performance; greater satisfaction with a service or product leads to greater use of it.

If output attributes change, then user satisfaction will also change (see previous indicator). And if satisfaction levels change, this affects the amount the service will be used. An example of the indicator is the average amount of use of reference services per year by those who are very satisfied with the quality of reference services.

Figure 3.8

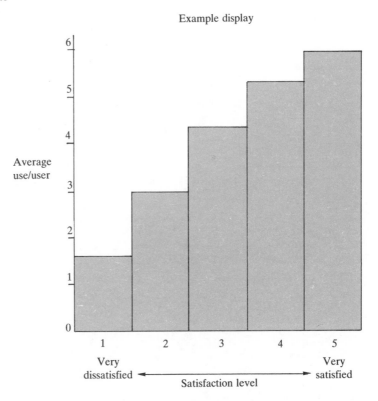

The example in Figure 3.8 shows a very useful relationship: the use of a library service increases with higher levels of satisfaction. Use falls off appreciably with low satisfaction. Thus, managers can establish the effect of performance improvement on the extent to which services are used. Section 6.4 gives an even more sophisticated relationship among several output attributes.

Internal comparison	Internal comparisons can be performed at several levels.

Internal comparisons can be performed at several levels.

First is a comparison of the average amount of use by satisfaction levels over time to determine whether the relationship between use and satisfaction is changing or not.

Secondly, we can compare the average amount of use of a particular service as the levels of a single output attribute vary. For example, we can compare the average annual amount of use for those very satisfied with the reference service and for those very dissatisfied with the reference service. This gives an indication of the impact of quality on the performance of the reference service.

Thirdly, we can examine the average amount a particular service is used according to levels of satisfaction with each service attribute. For example, compare the average annual use of the reference service for those very satisfied with the quality of the service, with the timeliness of the service, with the availability of the service etc. This comparison gives an indication how sensitive amount of use is to the different attributes of the service. The information can help decide which attributes to focus attention on.

Fourthly, we can compare the average amount of use per level of attribute across services. For example, we can compare the average annual amount of use by those who are very satisfied with the reference service, the interlibrary lending service etc. This comparison can help the library manager to decide which service to focus attention on, particularly when allocating limited resources.

External comparison

External comparisons of this indicator are not very useful.

How to improve *Amount of use by satisfaction levels*

- Increase awareness through promotion
- Identify and respond to user needs and requirements
- Improve attributes of service that are important to the user
- Develop an understanding of user expectations
- Increase, improve or reallocate resources
- Expand or change hours of service
- Increase the number of service locations
- Expand means of access to the service.

3.4 Cost-effectiveness indicators

Cost-effectiveness relates the users' view of service or product performance (that is, effectiveness) to the cost of the resources necessary to provide the product or the service.

The indicator parallels the operational performance indicators which relate outputs produced (from the library's perspective) to the input costs. Both types of indicators are, in a sense, return-on-investment indicators but seen from different perspectives. Cost-effectiveness indicators demonstrate the return on investment from the funder's perspective. All the cost-effectiveness indicators are derived from combinations of input costs and effectiveness measures.

Four cost-effectiveness indicators have been defined:

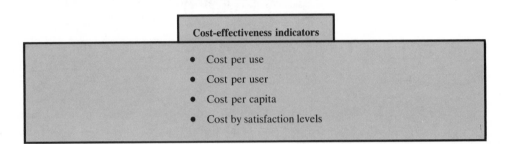

Cost-effectiveness indicators

- Cost per use
- Cost per user
- Cost per capita
- Cost by satisfaction levels

The *Cost per use* indicator relates the amount of use made of a service to the cost of resources needed to provide the service. Often the same as *Cost per output, Cost per use* can be used to identify which service is providing the greatest return on investment. The lower the *Cost per use* the better the performance.

We can invert this indicator to calculate the amount of use per unit of resources (monetary cost, hours of staff time etc). This allows us to predict the change in amount of use that could result from the addition or subtraction of resources.

Figure 3.9

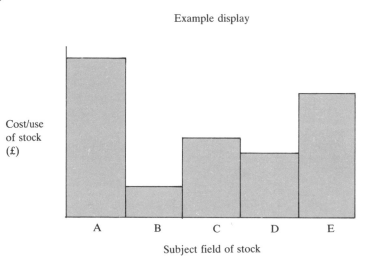

Example display

The example display in Figure 3.9 shows average cost per use of stock for several subject fields (it could be other classes of stock as well, for example, fiction, non-fiction, reference). Library managers can identify areas in which *Cost per use* is high, that is, subject fields A and E above, and determine why such costs appear out-of-line. There may be valid reasons such as price of documents being high for some field. On the other hand, in-depth analysis may reveal ways of reducing *Cost per use*.

Internal comparison

The most obvious comparison is of *Cost per use* across services. This comparison indicates how a library's resources are benefiting the users. A service which has an especially high *Cost per use* should be reviewed to determine whether there are valid reasons for the high average *Cost per use*. A high average cost could be the result of an inefficient allocation of resources (for example tasks being performed by over-qualified staff). High average costs alone are not necessarily sufficient grounds to discontinue a service. A second comparison is of the *Cost per use* of the service over time.

External comparison

By comparing your library's *Cost per use* indicator with those of other libraries you can determine whether the *Cost per use* for a particular service is 'good' or not. On the whole, a library with a low *Cost per use* for a service is performing better than a library with a high *Cost per use* for the same service. However, if the way the service itself is defined and run, the definition and method of measurement of use, and the definition and measurement of cost differ, the comparison may not be valid.

How to lower *Cost per use*

- Reduce input costs
- Change policies
- Change procedures
- Batch activities if possible
- Improve attributes of service that are important to users
- Increase, improve or reallocate resources.

The *Cost per user* indicator relates the number of users of a service to the costs of providing the service and the lower the *Cost per user* the better the library's performance.

Note the distinction between this indicator and the indicator discussed next, *Cost per capita*. *Cost per user* only concerns people who actually use a service, a service location, or the entire library. It does not include the potential users in the population to be served. On the other hand, *Cost per capita* includes all potential users – that is, the population served.

It is useful to compare *Cost per user* where numbers of users vary because evidence shows that, for some services, it costs more per user to serve small populations than large ones. This has implications for decisions concerning branch libraries.

The example in Figure 3.10 displays *Cost per user* of a service or library for which hours of availability vary. This indicator suggests the value of increased hours of availability. In a previous example we showed that total amount of use (and average amount of use) increases as hours of availability increase. Presumably the number of users also goes up with increased availability since, for example, some users may be able to visit the library and use its services only at odd times. Average cost per use may decrease gradually as hours of availability increase, up to a point, and then increase rapidly, because costs may be higher for weekend or night service, and the additional number of users may be small for those time periods. Thus, *Cost per use* might increase with increased hours of availability above, for example 70 hours of availability.

Internal comparison

The *Cost per user* indicator can be compared for a specific service over time. This will reflect any changes in input costs or number of users. The *Cost per user* can also be compared internally across services to see how resources needed relate to the number of users. This indicator should be used in conjunction with the *Cost per use* indicator for a more complete picture of the relative costs of services.

The *Cost per user* can also be compared for various services across service locations. Locations with a high *Cost per user* for a specific service should be investigated in more depth to determine the reasons for either a high cost or low use of that service.

External comparison

An external comparison of the *Cost per user* indicator should be performed in conjunction with a comparison of the indicators *Cost per use* and *Users as a proportion of population*. Care must be taken to ensure that the same cost elements are included in the measurement of costs. The comparisons can help the library

Figure 3.10

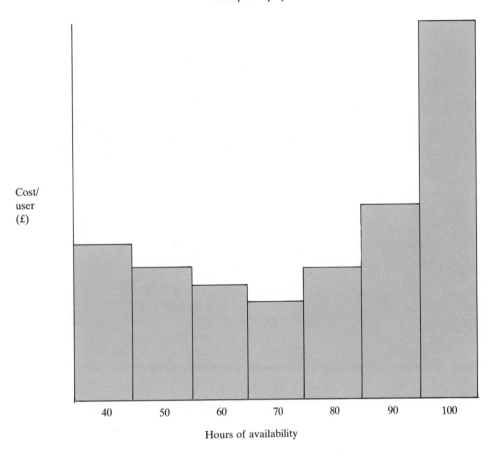

Example display

Cost/
user
(£)

Hours of availability

manager determine whether the input costs are at a 'reasonable' level for the number of users served.

How to improve *Cost per user*

- Improve attributes of service that are important to users and non-users
- Increase, improve or reallocate resources
- Increase awareness through promotion
- Increase service locations
- Increase access to library and services (for example improve parking)
- Increase availability (for example open more or different hours)
- Identify unmet needs and target services to meet them.

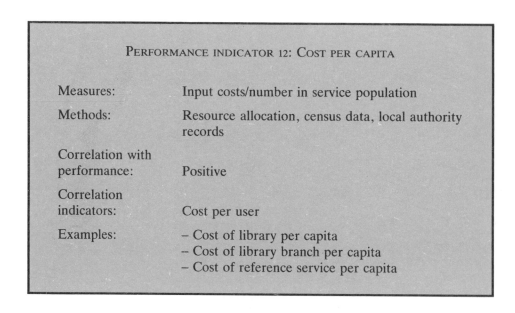

PERFORMANCE INDICATOR 12: COST PER CAPITA

Measures: Input costs/number in service population

Methods: Resource allocation, census data, local authority records

Correlation with performance: Positive

Correlation indicators: Cost per user

Examples:
– Cost of library per capita
– Cost of library branch per capita
– Cost of reference service per capita

The *Cost per capita* indicator relates the library's resources to the population it serves. The assumption underlying this indicator is that the higher the cost per capita, the better the library is performing (or the library's funders are performing). However, this assumes that the *Cost per use* is always the same across the libraries being compared, otherwise the indicator could be negatively correlated with performance. It is seen as an indicator of the investment being made on behalf of the population served.

Figure 3.11

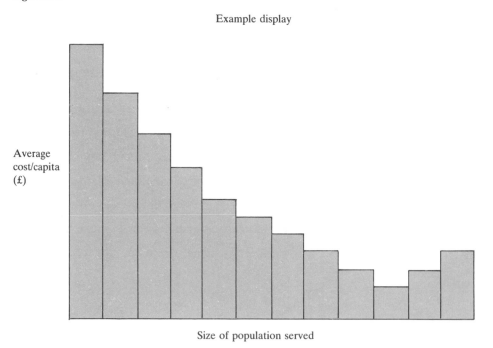

Example display

Average cost/capita (£)

Size of population served

In the example in Figure 3.11 library cost per capita decreases as size of population increases (up to a point). There are several explanations for this relationship. The most obvious is that economies of scale affect costs up to a 'critical mass' (see Appendix A). However, this effect may occur even when economies of scale are taken into account.

Demand for public library services may depend partly on clusters of people with shared information or library needs. People of similar age, education or ethnic background tend to live or work in the same areas. These clusters are most common in large, populated areas and, per capita, it is less expensive to serve large groups. We need more stock per person to serve a small group; and we should bear this in mind when budgeting for branch libraries in areas of various sizes.

Internal comparison

The *Cost per capita* indicator can be compared:

- internally over time to monitor the investment in the library or specific services and products of the library over time
- across services to determine the relative costs of services
- across service locations to determine the relative costs of services at different locations.

External comparison

The *Cost per capita* indicator can be compared across libraries to indicate the relative investment in the library or its services and products. Take care that the same definition of 'number in the service population' is used and that the same cost elements are included.

How to improve *Cost per capita*

- Increase funding
- Promote library services
- Increase, improve, reallocate or change resources
- Develop an understanding of the consequences of library use.

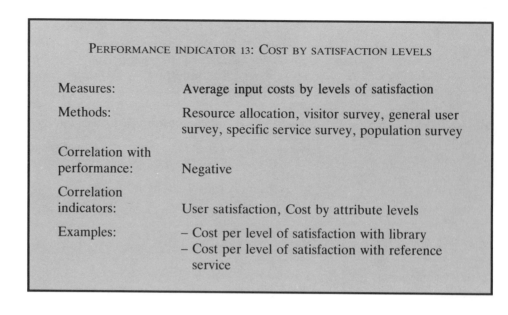

PERFORMANCE INDICATOR 13: COST BY SATISFACTION LEVELS

Measures:	**Average input costs by levels of satisfaction**
Methods:	Resource allocation, visitor survey, general user survey, specific service survey, population survey
Correlation with performance:	Negative
Correlation indicators:	User satisfaction, Cost by attribute levels
Examples:	– Cost per level of satisfaction with library – Cost per level of satisfaction with reference service

The *Cost by satisfaction levels* indicator relates the cost of resources to provide a service and the satisfaction of users with that service. It is similar to *Cost by attribute levels*, except from the users' perspective.

Cost by satisfaction levels is useful in helping the library manager to understand the resource implications of improving the output of a service. For example, the indicator can be used to predict:

● what resources would be necessary to increase satisfaction with quality of a service

● the effect on satisfaction of changing the resources allocated to the service.

The lower the cost is to provide higher satisfaction, the better the performance.

Figure 3.12

Example display

Average input costs by level of satisfaction is similar to *Cost by attribute levels*. Thus, another kind of display is given in the example in Figure 3.12. Here average cost is given for two methods of service provision, for example screened online search output and non-screened output, across levels of satisfaction. Method B is less expensive than Method A at low levels of satisfaction but more at high levels of satisfaction. If high satisfaction is important then Method A is superior, even though overall average costs could be greater for Method A.

Internal comparison

The internal comparison of costs and satisfaction can be performed at three levels:

- the cost per level of satisfaction over time
- the average costs across levels of satisfaction, for example the costs for very satisfied *versus* costs for very dissatisfied
- the cost per level of satisfaction across services. This can help to decide which services to focus attention on.

External comparison

The external comparison of this indicator is not particularly useful.

How to improve *Cost by satisfaction levels*

- Increase, improve or reallocate resources
- Improve attributes of service that are important to the user
- Identify and respond to user needs and requirements
- Develop an understanding of user expectations.

3.5 Impact indicators

Impact indicators help to answer the question: is the library achieving what it set out to achieve? They relate the library and information needs of the population served to the amount of use made of the library and its services and products.

Three impact indicators have been defined:

Impact indicators
• Users as a proportion of population
• Use per capita
• Needs fill rate

PERFORMANCE INDICATOR 14: USERS AS A PROPORTION OF POPULATION

Measures:	Number of users/number in service population
Methods:	Library records, visitor survey, general user survey, specific service survey, population survey, census data, local authority records
Correlation with performance:	Positive
Related indicators:	Turnover rate, Use per capita
Examples:	– Proportion of the population registered as borrowers – Proportion of housebound that receive service

The *Users as a proportion of population* indicator relates the number of users of a service or product to the number of potential users of the service or the population served. An example is the proportion of the service population that is registered as borrowers of a library. (Note that this is the PLA output measure: Registrations as a percentage of the population.) Another example is the proportion of the housebound in the library's service area that actually receives library service.

The relationship of this indicator with performance is positive as the greater the proportion of the service population actually served, the better the performance of the library. The indicator can be used to set objectives for the library and to indicate the impact of the library in the community.

Figure 3.13

Example display

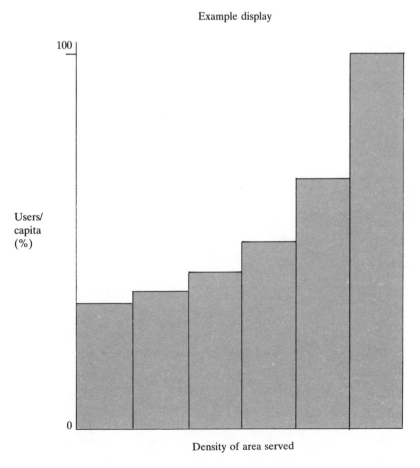

Density of area served

The *Use per capita* indicator is displayed by population density of area served. This indicator has implications for locating branch libraries.

Internal comparison

The indicator can be compared over time to monitor change. The proportion of the service population that uses a service can be compared across services to indicate which services are actually reaching the target population.

External comparison

This indicator lends itself well to external comparison because libraries serving large populations can be compared directly with libraries serving small populations.

A comparison of the overall impact of a library with other libraries does indicate how well each library is performing relative to the others. However, when the comparison is done service-by-service the performance of each library reflects the service priorities of that library so comparisons may not be as direct.

How to improve *Users as a proportion of population*

- Improve attributes of service that are important to users and non-users
- Identify and respond to the needs and requirements of the population
- Develop an understanding of expectations of library services
- Increase awareness through promotion
- Increase service locations
- Increase access to the library and services
- Increase availability of library and services.

The amount a library service or product is used is often considered an indicator of performance. However, in keeping with the definitions of performance presented in the previous section, it is difficult to know just how to interpret the meaning of 'amount of use' across libraries without some normalising measure. The most common normalising measure is population served (also referred to as 'domain measure' – see Section 2).

If Library A has 100,000 people in its service community and handles 10,000 reference enquiries in a year, and Library B has 30,000 people and handles 5,000 reference enquiries in the same year, the amount of *Use per capita* gives a more comparable result than the number of reference enquiries alone. Library A has 0.10 reference enquiries per capita and Library B has 0.17 reference enquiries per capita. Thus, while Library A is dealing with twice as many absolute reference enquiries, Library B is actually doing more reference work for its community than Library A.

A second normalising factor is amount of resources used (input measure). The relationship between input resources used and number of uses is covered in Section 3.4, Cost-effectiveness indicators.

The relationship of *Use per capita* with performance is a positive one. The greater the *Use per capita*, the better the library performance.

The example in Figure 3.14 displays the relative impact or success among services provided by a library or libraries.

Internal comparison

Once we have measured the amount of use over a specified period of time, we can set objectives for improving the amount of use in the future. By repeating the measure over the same period of time at regular intervals we can monitor progress.

The Use per capita can also be compared:

- across services to determine the relative success of the services

- across service locations to determine the relative success of services at each location.

For all these comparisons the number in the service population needs to be defined carefully for comparability. Use either the entire service population of the library or the population that could potentially use a service provided by the library (that is, a subset of the entire service population). Reasons for low *Use per capita* should be explored.

External comparison

Comparing the amount of use of a service or product across libraries is more complex:

Figure 3.14

Example display

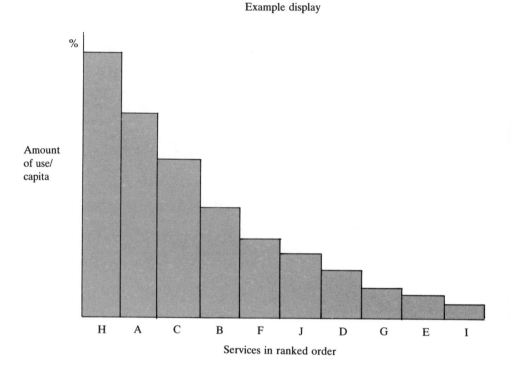

- First, it is important that the libraries being compared use the same definition for what is to be counted as a reference enquiry (all enquiries, all excluding direction enquiries, all enquiries from visitors but not telephone enquiries, all enquiries taking 5 minutes or more to respond to etc);

- Secondly, the reference enquiries need to be counted over the same or similar period of time;

- Thirdly, the enquiries should be counted in the same way (all enquiries logged over the time period, all enquiries logged over a sample time period, or a sample of enquiries logged over the time period).

If all these conditions exist the indicators are comparable across libraries.

You may compare the *Use per capita* of a specific service across libraries for the subsets of the populations of the libraries' service areas (for example the housebound). But you should also compare *Users as a proportion* of population to gain a clearer understanding of the relative success of the libraries.

How to increase *Use per capita*

- Improve attributes of service that are important to the user

- Identify unmet needs and target services to meet them

- Increase awareness through promotion

- Expand or change hours of service

- Increase the number of service locations

- Expand means of access to the service.

The *Needs fill rate* indicator can be used at two levels:

- Relate needs satisfied and needs identified for users of the library's services and products — This includes a set of indicators often referred to as 'fill rates' (for example, the PLA Output Measures: browsing, author, title and subject fill rates). Examples include the number of needed items (titles) found divided by the number of items (titles) needed (or title fill rate).

- Relate the extent of need in the service population to the proportion of these needs that were/are met by the library, and by alternative sources — This is much harder to do than the first level. Part of the problem is defining 'needs'. However, studies of the information needs of populations have been conducted. The information needs of special subpopulations are somewhat easier to determine because the subpopulations tend to be relatively small, although definitional problems still remain.

The relationship of *Needs fill rate* to performance is positive. The higher the fill rate the better the performance of the library.

Titles found divided by titles needed is an example of the fill rate relationship (Figure 3.15). This indicator is a useful tool for assessing collection development needs for various subject fields (or other types of stock).

Internal comparison

Compare the *Needs fill rate*:

- over time to monitor changes

- across services to determine the relative success of the various services in meeting needs. Reasons for low fill rates should be investigated further

- across service locations to determine how successful the services at each location are in meeting needs. As before, reasons for low fill rates should be investigated further.

External comparison

An external comparison of *Needs fill rate* across libraries does provide the library manager with information about how well the library is performing relative to others. However, it is important that the needs are defined and measured in the same way. This comparison can help the library manager make decisions about which services need further attention.

Figure 3.15

Example display

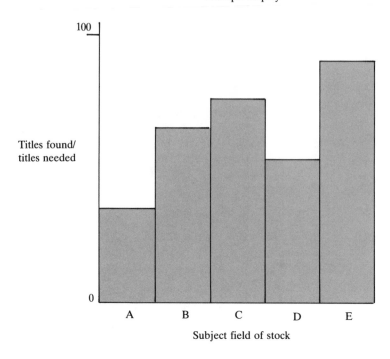

Titles found/
titles needed

Subject field of stock

How to improve *Needs fill rate*

- Identify unmet needs and target services and programmes to meet them
- Increase awareness of the library and its services through promotion
- Expand means of access to the service
- Expand or change hours of service
- Increase the number of service locations
- Increase, improve or reallocate resources.

3.6 An example of relationships between measures

Below is an example to demonstrate how relationships between measures can reveal useful management information. In this example, assume that library staff are observed for a period of two weeks and that 50 staff members spend anywhere between one and 50 hours providing a service (for example interlibrary loan) or operational function (for example acquisitions). The hypothetical results of staff hours worked and the number of units of output produced by the 50 staff members are shown in Table 3.2.

Table 3.2 Example of values for determining relationships between staff input and output: 50 staff members observed over two weeks

Hours worked (x)	Units produced (y)		Hours worked (x)	Units produced (y)
18	102		31	121
19	116		10	25
48	345		43	231
8	28		36	191
25	140		14	65
29	182		24	121
4	12		2	1
46	281		47	265
37	235		32	146
12	46		12	36
16	68		17	60
34	210		35	190
36	230		41	211
7	21		5	17
44	270		24	121
27	138		27	140
6	16		1	2
42	211		22	76
38	268		33	185
19	128		16	61
29	195		13	45
34	205		46	210
50	340		45	260
2	5		3	4
23	136		22	75
653	**3,928**	**Total**	**601**	**2,859**

The total number of hours worked by these 50 staff members during the two-week period is 1,254 hours and they produced 6,787 transactions or units. Neither of these two measures has much meaning alone; nor do averages of hours per staff member (25.1 hours per person) or units per staff member (135.74 units per person).

However, relating the two measures as average number of units produced per hour has some useful meaning (5.41 units per hour). If the number of units produced by the library or libraries is increasing each year from about 176,000 units in 1989 to 220,000 in 1990 the library or libraries must budget for about 8,133 more hours to do the work, that is, 44,000 additional units divided by 5.41 units per hour. Or if the average hourly wage is £6.00, the budget increase would be about £48,800.

The relationship can be displayed in graphic as well as tabular form as shown in Figure 3.16. Again, the data displayed as such do not convey a great deal of meaning. Using linear regression the relationship provides some more quantitative information through the following equation:

$$y = a + bx$$
$$= -25 + 6.4x$$

where y is units produced and x is number of hours worked. This equation is represented in the graph by a straight line. Using the equation we can estimate the number of units we could expect from a staff member working 1–50 hours in a two-week period. For example if somebody works 60 hours, we would expect that person to produce about 360 units. In addition, we can assess an individual's work to see whether the staff member's productivity is above the line (good) or below it (bad).

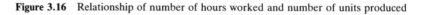

Figure 3.16 Relationship of number of hours worked and number of units produced

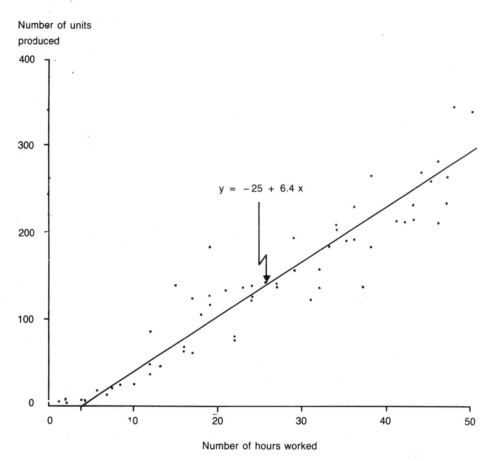

However, there is more information in the data than revealed by the relationship expressed by mere average. For example, by grouping the data by ranges of hours worked as shown below, we find that the staff are much more productive if they work more heavily on the service (Figure 3.17).

For instance, the staff working less than 10 hours on the service over two weeks only produce an average of 2.73 units per hour. If they work 11 to 20 hours they produce an average of 4.66 units per hour, and this trend continues all the way up to 5.81 units per hour for those who work 41 to 50 hours. This relationship (indicator) given by the hypothetical example is not unusual for library services or operational functions. Given such knowledge, library managers can improve productivity by centralising services or batching services. If this can be done for the entire year (1989 in the example), the work can be done in about 29,830 hours instead of 32,600 hours, thus saving £16,600.

Factors – such as the number of years for which an individual has worked in this field – can contribute to productivity as well. In the hypothetical example, this attribute is distinguished by the two columns of numbers where the first column is experienced staff and the second column is inexperienced staff. When productivity is calculated by level of experience for the amount of time worked, experienced staff average 6.02 units per hour and inexperienced staff average 4.76 units per hour.

Figure 3.17

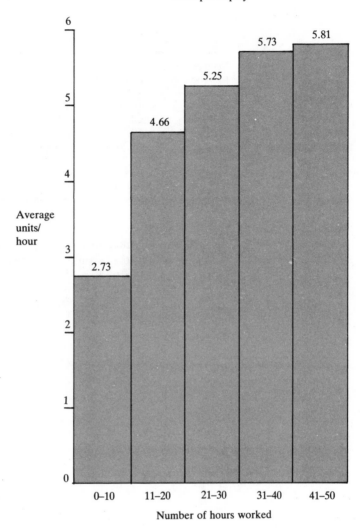

Example display

Average units/hour

Number of hours worked

Table 3.3 Average productivity of experienced and inexperienced staff

Number of hours worked	Experienced	Inexperienced	All
0–10	3.04	2.33	2.73
11–20	5.48	3.71	4.66
21–30	5.95	4.48	5.25
31–40	6.41	4.99	5.73
41–50	6.29	5.30	5.81
All	**6.02**	**4.76**	**5.41**

Thus, experienced staff would appear to be more productive and this is true at all levels of amount of work. However, an important question is whether it costs experienced staff more per unit since they are paid more. If experienced staff are paid £7.00 per hour and inexperienced staff £5.00 per hour the cost per unit produced for experienced staff is £1.16 per unit (£7.00 per hour divided by 6.02 units per hour), and the cost per unit for inexperienced staff is £1.05 per unit (£5.00 per hour divided by 4.76 units per hour).

Consequently, it would cost slightly less for inexperienced staff to do the work. Overall it would cost about £19,800 less per year to have all the work done by inexperienced staff. The total cost of producing 176,000 units based on the calculated productivity levels by levels of experience and number of hours worked are as follows:

Table 3.4   Cost to produce 176,000 units by experienced and inexperienced staff

Number of hours worked	Experienced	Inexperienced	All
0–10	£405,300	£377,700	£386,800
11–20	224,800	237,200	226,600
21–30	207,100	196,400	201,100
31–40	192,200	176,400	184,300
41–50	195,900	166,000	181,800
All	**£204,700**	**£184,900**	**£195,200**

If quality and timeliness are equal for the two levels of staff, the optimum management strategy would be to have the work batched and done by inexperienced staff at a £5.00 hourly wage.

Section 4. Examples of performance indicators for library services and operational functions

4.1 Introduction

So far we have looked at performance measures (Section 2) and performance indicators (Section 3). In each case we have outlined at least one practical application.

In this section, we look at performance measurement from the library managers' perspective. Suppose, for example, we wish to assess the performance of inter-library lending – which indicators and measures are appropriate? Which would be best for evaluating services to special groups?

The manual is not long enough to present all the indicators appropriate to each system or service we may wish to monitor. Rather we take a set of services which affect users directly, and identify the indicators and their related measures appropriate for each:

- access to library facilities/premises

- access to library stock

- access to library equipment

- interlibrary lending

- reference and information services

- services to special groups

- activities.

We add one example of an operational function, acquisitions. The operational functions are essential to serving users but they have no direct involvement with the users. These examples should assist you to work out the:

- attributes

- input measures

- output measures

- operational performance indicators

- effectiveness indicators

- cost-effectiveness indicators

- impact indicators

that you could best use to evaluate performance in all areas of your own service or library.

To find details of measures, refer to the list at the beginning of Section 2; for indicators, refer to the list in Section 3.1. Guidance on how to obtain measures and indicators appears in Sections 5 and 6 and Appendix A.

4.2 Access to library facilities/premises

Usually, when people use a public library, they use a specific service. Sometimes, though, they may need access to specific facilities of the library. An example of this type of use is a room in the library which may be used for a meeting organised by an outside group. Or someone may visit the library to check a notice-board, or to pick up a leaflet. How do we judge the performance of the library in allowing people access for these purposes?

Service input cost measures
- Amount of resources — See Section 2.2 for details of facilities/premises costs.

Service output measures
- Amount (quantity) of facilities — See Section 2.2.
- Quality of facilities — This measure could include quality of architecture, attractiveness, quality of lighting, heating etc.
- Availability of library — This measure is of the number of hours the library is open for service over a specified period of time.
- Accessibility of library — This measure can be of the average distance or time necessary to travel to the library by users visiting the library over a specified period of time. It can also be a measure of the physical access features of the library including access for the disabled, parking etc.

Service effectiveness measures
- Number of visits, number of uses of facilities
- Number of visitors
- Amount of use of the library
- Purpose of use of the library.

Operational performance indicators
- Cost per square metre of space
- Average cost/level of availability
- Average cost/level of accessibility.

Effectiveness indicators
- User satisfaction with and importance of availability of the library
- User satisfaction with and importance of accessibility of the library
- Average amount of use/level of user satisfaction
- Average number of visits/level of user satisfaction
- Average number of visitors/level of user satisfaction
- Average frequency of use/level of availability
- Average number of visits/level of availability
- Average number of visitors/level of availability
- Average frequency of use/level of accessibility
- Average number of visits/level of accessibility
- Average number of visitors/level of accessibility.

Cost-effectiveness indicators
- Cost per visit
- Cost per visitor
- Cost per capita
- Average cost/level of satisfaction.

Impact indicators
- Number of visits/number of visitors.

4.3 Access to library stock One of the most important services offered by a library to the community it serves is access to the stock.

Service input cost measures

- Amount of resources — This measure includes any one or more of the cost measures associated with stock resources. (See Section 2.2 for more details).

- Cost of stock lending (issues and/or interlibrary loan) — This measure includes the costs associated with the actual lending of stock. It could include any allocation of staff, space, equipment, supplies, administration etc that relate to the lending process.

- Cost of reshelving — This measure includes the cost of reshelving materials that have been used. As above, it could include the allocation of staff, space, equipment, supplies, administration etc associated with the reshelving process.

Service output measures

- Number of items in stock — See Section 2.2.

- Number of titles in stock — See Section 2.2.

- Timeliness of loans — This is a measure of the time taken to have an item issued. For items issued directly to the user the timeliness is measured by the actual time to process the loan plus any time the user spent waiting to be served. For items loaned through interlibrary loan the timeliness is measured as the length of time between a request being received by the library and the requested item (or a message indicating that the item is unavailable) being sent to the requesting library.

- Scope of stock — This is a measure of the extent to which various subject areas are covered by the stock. It can be measured either by comparing the library's stock against a predetermined list of titles, or by having an expert rate the library's collection to a standard.

- Comprehensiveness of stock — This is a measure of the extent to which all possible subject areas are covered by the stock, and the depth of coverage of each subject area. This can be measured by having a subject expert assess the library's collection in that subject area to a standard.

- Availability of stock — This is a measure of the hours during which the stock is available.

- Accessibility of stock — Stock can be inaccessible because of remote storage, compact storage, items being mis-shelved, used in the library, on loan, missing etc. Measures include the proportion of stock that is directly accessible by users, and the average time taken to access an item of stock. It could also include proportion of items mis-shelved.

Service effectiveness measures

- Number of items of stock used

- Number of titles of stock used

- Number of users of stock

- Frequency of use of stock

- Purpose of use of stock.

Operational performance indicators

- Cost per item

- Cost per title

- Cost per level of availability of stock

- Cost per level of scope of stock

- Cost per level of comprehensiveness of stock

- Cost per level of accessibility of stock.

Effectiveness indicators	
	• User satisfaction with and importance of timeliness of loans
	• User satisfaction with and importance of availability of stock
	• User satisfaction with and importance of scope of stock
	• User satisfaction with and importance of comprehensiveness of stock
	• User satisfaction with and importance of accessibility of stock
	• Number of items of stock used/number of items in stock (item turnover rate)
	• Number of titles of stock used/number of titles in stock (title turnover rate)
	• Number of users of stock at various distances from library
	• Average number of items of stock used/level of user satisfaction
	• Average number of users of stock/level of user satisfaction
	• Average frequency of use of stock/level of user satisfaction
	• Average number of items of stock used/level of availability
	• Average frequency of use of stock/level of availability
	• Average number of items of stock used/level of scope of stock
	• Average number of users of stock/level of scope of stock
	• Average frequency of use of stock/level of scope of stock
	• Average number of items of stock used/level of comprehensiveness of stock
	• Average number of users of stock/level of comprehensiveness of stock
	• Average frequency of use of stock/level of comprehensiveness of stock
	• Average number of items of stock used/level of accessibility of stock
	• Average number of users of stock/level of accessibility of stock
	• Average frequency of use of stock/level of accessibility of stock.

Cost-effectiveness indicators	
	• Cost per item of stock used
	• Cost per title of stock used
	• Cost per user of stock
	• Cost of stock per capita
	• Average cost/level of user satisfaction with stock attributes.

Impact indicators	
	• Number of items sought by specific author/number of items found by specific author
	• Number of specific titles sought/number of specific titles found
	• Number of subject items sought/number of subject items found
	• Number of items sought by browsing/number of items found by browsing
	• Number of items of stock used per capita
	• Number of titles of stock used per capita
	• Number of users of stock per capita.

Other derived indicators	
	• Number of items of stock used/number of titles of stock used
	• Number of items borrowed on interlibrary loan/number of items in stock.

4.4 Access to library equipment

Libraries can provide their users with direct access to several different kinds of equipment for stand-alone use. Examples include photocopiers, typewriters, microcomputers. Access to these pieces of equipment constitutes a distinct service which the library provides. Note that we do not include in this section equipment such as online public access catalogue (OPAC) terminals because they are used as part of the access to stock service.

Service input cost measures

- Amount of resources — This measure includes any one of the cost measures associated with equipment/systems resource (see Section 2.2 for more details).

Service output measures

- Amount (quantity) of equipment — This is a measure of the number of items or pieces of equipment provided to users.

- Reliability of equipment — This can be measured as:
  – the proportion of time the equipment cannot be used because of a failure;
  – the mean time between failures.

- Availability of equipment — This is a measure of the hours the equipment is available over a specified period of time.

- Accessibility of equipment — Equipment may be inaccessible to a user when needed because it is in use, out of order, being repaired etc. Measures include the proportion of time the equipment is in use over a specified time period, and the average time users have to wait to gain access to the equipment they need.

Service effectiveness measures

- Number of uses of equipment

- Number of users of equipment

- Frequency of use of equipment

- Purpose of use of equipment.

Operational performance indicators

- Cost per equipment item

- Cost per level of reliability of equipment

- Cost per level of availability of equipment

- Cost per level of accessibility of equipment.

Effectiveness indicators

- User satisfaction with and importance of reliability of equipment

- User satisfaction with and importance of availability of equipment

- User satisfaction with and importance of accessibility of equipment

- Average number of users of equipment/level of user satisfaction

- Average amount of use of equipment/level of user satisfaction

- Average number of uses of equipment/level of user satisfaction

- Average number of users of equipment/level of availability

- Average frequency of use of equipment/level of availability

- Average number of uses of equipment/level of availability

- Average number of users of equipment/level of accessibility

- Average frequency of use of equipment/level of accessibility

- Average number of uses of equipment/level of accessibility.

Cost-effectiveness indicators	• Cost per use of equipment
	• Cost per user of equipment
	• Cost of equipment per capita
	• Average cost/level of user satisfaction.
Impact indicators	• Number of uses of equipment per capita
	• Number of uses of equipment/number of users of equipment.

4.5 Interlibrary borrowing	Interlibrary borrowing is separated here from interlibrary lending (which was included in Section 4.2 on access to stock). Interlibrary borrowing is a service which supplements a library's stock.

Service input cost measures

- Amount of resources — This measure includes the cost associated with interlibrary borrowing. It can include any allocation of staff, space, equipment, supplies, administration etc that relates to the interlibrary borrowing process.

Service output measures

- Numbers of items requested in interlibrary borrowing — This is a measure of the number of items requested from other libraries over a specified time period.

- Number of interlibrary borrowing requests sent — This is a measure of the number of requests for materials sent to other libraries over a specified period of time. It recognises that several items can be requested from a library in one request transaction.

- Timeliness of interlibrary borrowing — This can be measured in two ways. First is the elapsed time between a user placing a request and receiving the requested item. Second is the difference between when the request was needed and when it was actually received.

- Quality of items borrowed — Quality of interlibrary borrowing can refer to photocopy quality, accuracy of fulfilment etc.

- Availability of interlibrary borrowing — Whether such borrowing is done and availability of staff to provide this service.

Service effectiveness measures

- Number of items borrowed
- Number of users of interlibrary borrowing
- Amount of use of interlibrary borrowing
- Purpose of use of interlibrary borrowing.

Operational performance indicators

- Cost per item borrowed
- Cost per interlibrary borrowing request sent
- Average cost per level of timeliness of interlibrary borrowing.

Effectiveness indicators

- User satisfaction with and importance of timeliness of interlibrary borrowing
- Proportion of items borrowed within various time-frames
- Average number of interlibrary borrowing requests/level of user satisfaction.

Cost-effectiveness indicators

- Cost per item requested in interlibrary borrowing
- Cost per user of interlibrary borrowing
- Cost of interlibrary borrowing per capita
- Average cost/level of user satisfaction.

Impact indicators

- Number of items borrowed from other libraries/number of items requested from other libraries
- Number of items requested from other libraries/number of interlibrary borrowing requests sent

- Number of items borrowed from other libraries/number of users of interlibrary borrowing

- Number of items requested from other libraries/number of users of interlibrary borrowing

- Number of items borrowed per capita

- Number of interlibrary borrowing requests per capita.

4.6 Reference and information services

Reference and information services are increasingly important library services as information resources proliferate. They can range from handling straightforward directional enquiries and ready reference enquiries to very complex enquiries which require searches of online databases or other reference tools.

Service input cost measures

- Amount of resources of reference and information services — This measure includes the cost of providing reference and information services. It can include an allocation of staff, space, equipment, supplies etc associated with provision of the service.

- Amount of resources of online database searching — This is a measure of the costs associated with online database searching including staff, equipment, database subscription and use charges, database access (telecommunications) charges etc.

Service output measures

- Number of reference and information enquiries received — This is a measure of the number of reference and information enquiries received over a specified period of time.

- Number of reference and information enquiries filled — This is a measure of the number of reference and information enquiries that are answered over a specified period of time.

- Number of online searches performed — This is a measure of the number of online searches performed in pursuit of a reference or information enquiry. The user may have asked for the search, or library staff may have deemed it the best way to address the enquiry. Note that the definition of an online search can vary considerably. Search definitions range from the entire amount of searching that must be done to respond to a user enquiry, to the application of a search strategy to a single database.

- Number of references retrieved by online search — This is the total number of bibliographic references retrieved through an online search. Again, the definition of retrieved references can vary from the number of references identified by searching to the number of selected/screened/evaluated references presented to the user.

- Accuracy of the reference response — This measure of the correctness of the response given to the enquiry is obtained through expert rating on a predetermined scale.

- Comprehensiveness of the reference response — The completeness of the response given to the enquiry. It is measured through expert rating on a predetermined scale.

- Level of complexity of the reference response — This is a measure of the level of complexity/comprehension of the reference response. Some users want very simple responses, others want highly technical responses to their enquiries. This can be measured through expert rating to a standard.

- Relevance of the reference response — The appropriateness of the response given to an enquiry. Sometimes information may appear to be relevant to an enquiry but may actually not be. This measure can be obtained through expert or user rating to a standard.

- Timeliness of the reference response — This can be measured in two ways. First is the time between a user making an enquiry and receiving a response. Second is the time between a user's indication of when a response is needed and when the response is actually received.

- Availability of the reference and information services — This measure is of the hours during which the reference and information services are available.

- Accessibility of the reference and information services — This measure is the proportion of time the reference and information services were accessible when needed. It can also be measured as the average time a user must wait to be served.

Service effectiveness measures

- Amount of use of the reference and information services
- Purpose of use of the reference and information services.

Operational performance indicators

- Cost per enquiry filled
- Cost per online search
- Cost per reference retrieved
- Average cost per level of timeliness of response
- Average cost per level of accuracy of response
- Average cost per level of comprehensiveness of the response
- Average cost per level of complexity of the response
- Average cost per level of relevance of the response
- Average cost per level of availability of the reference and information services
- Average cost per level of accessibility of the reference and information services.

Effectiveness indicators

- User satisfaction with timeliness of the response
- User satisfaction with accuracy of the response
- User satisfaction with comprehensiveness of the response
- User satisfaction with level of complexity of the response
- User satisfaction with relevance of the response
- User satisfaction with number of references retrieved
- User satisfaction with availability of the reference and information services
- User satisfaction with accessibility of the reference and information services
- Average number of reference enquiries made/level of user satisfaction
- Average number of users of the reference and information services/level of user satisfaction
- Average frequency of use of the reference and information services/level of user satisfaction
- Average number of reference enquiries made/level of availability
- Average number of users of the reference and information services/level of availability
- Average frequency of use of the reference and information services/level of availability
- Average number of reference enquiries made/level of accessibility
- Average number of users of the reference and information services/level of accessibility
- Average frequency of use of the reference and information services/level of accessibility.

Cost-effectiveness indicators	• Cost per enquiry received
	• Cost per use of the reference and information service
	• Cost per user of the reference and information service
	• Cost of reference and information services per capita
	• Average cost/level of user satisfaction
Impact indicators	• Number of reference enquiries received per capita
	• Number of reference enquiries filled per capita
	• Number of online searches performed per capita
	• Number of reference enquiries filled/number of reference enquiries received
Other derived indicators	• Number of online searches performed/number of reference enquiries filled

4.7 Services to special groups

Most public libraries offer services that are designed to meet the needs of special, targeted subsets of the population served. Such services are often called 'outreach services'. They are offered to the elderly, the institutionalised, the housebound, minority groups etc.

Service input cost measures

- Amount of resources — This measure includes the costs associated with the provision of services to special groups. These costs can include an allocation of staff, equipment, space, supplies, special materials, expenses, administration etc associated with the services.

Service output measures

- Number of services — This is a measure of the number of distinct services provided to special groups.

- Number of service points — This is a measure of the number of service points. It is an important measure (which affects costs) when several individuals can receive service from one service location, for example an old people's home.

- Frequency of service — This is a measure of the frequency with which the service is provided to individuals.

- Quality of service — This is a measure of the quality of the service provided to special groups. Measure of quality may vary according to the special group served. Quality is measured by expert rating on a predetermined scale. Measures might include relevance of materials provided, attentiveness, and so on.

- Timeliness of service — This is a measure of the responsiveness in time of service, which could be duration of time of service or the difference between time needed and time service is provided.

- Availability of service — This measure might be the number of hours staff actually have contact with service users.

- Accessibility of service — This measure includes proportion of times service is accessible, average distance to service, modes of access of service etc.

Service effectiveness measures

- Number of people served
- Number of service provisions
- Amount of use of the service
- Purpose of use of the service.

Operational performance indicators

- Cost per service
- Cost per service point
- Cost per service provision
- Average cost per level of frequency of service
- Average cost per level of quality of service.

Effectiveness indicators

- User satisfaction with frequency of service
- User satisfaction with quality of service
- Average number of people served/level of user satisfaction
- Average frequency of use of special service/level of user satisfaction
- Average number of people served/level of quality of service
- Average frequency of use of special service/level of quality of service

Cost-effectiveness indicators	• Cost per person served • Cost of special services per capita • Average cost/level of user satisfaction.
Impact indicators	• Number of people served per capita • Proportion of the target population reached.
Other derived indicators	• Number of people served per service point.

4.8 Activities

In addition to the range of services addressed above many public libraries organise activities for their users. Examples of these activities include children's story hour, book discussion groups, film shows. These activities may or may not actually take place in the library.

Service input cost measures

- Amount of resources — This is a measure of the costs associated with organising, preparing and presenting the activities. It can include an allocation of staff, space, equipment, supplies, expenses, administration etc associated with the activities.

Service output measures

- Number of activities held — This is a measure of the number of activities (events) held over a specified period of time. The same activity held several times should be counted each time it is held.

- Number of unique activities prepared — Each unique activity may be held/presented one or more times, but should be counted only once.

- Frequency of activities — This is a measure of the frequency with which activities are held.

- Quality of activities — This is measured by expert rating to a standard. It might include quality of presentation, materials provided etc.

- Timeliness of activities — This measure would include preparation time, notice time, programme time etc.

- Availability of activities — This would include the hours in which activities are provided.

- Accessibility of activities — This would be measured by average distance to activities, proportion of time activities are accessible when users want to attend etc.

Service effectiveness measures

- Number of people attending activities
- Frequency of attendance of activities
- Purpose of attendance at activities.

Operational performance indicators

- Cost per activity held
- Cost per unique activity prepared
- Average cost per level of frequency of activity
- Average cost per level of quality of activity.

Effectiveness indicators

- User satisfaction with frequency activity
- User satisfaction with quality of activity
- Number of unique activities prepared/number of activities held
- Number of people attending activities/number of activities held
- Number of people attending activities/number of unique activities prepared
- Average number of people attending activities/level of user satisfaction
- Average frequency of attendance/level of user satisfaction
- Average number of people attending activities/level of quality
- Average frequency of attendance/level of quality.

Cost-effectiveness indicators	• Cost per person attending activities
	• Cost per capita
	• Average cost of activities/level of user satisfaction.
Impact indicators	• Number of people attending activities per capita.

4.9 Operational functions
There are many operational functions in a public library that have a secondary effect on public library services and users. Such an example is acquisitions.

Operational function input cost measures

- Amount of resources — This is a measure of the staff, equipment, supplies and other costs associated with acquisitions.

Operational function output

- Quantities of acquisitions — This measure is of the number of titles acquired, number of items (or other materials, equipment etc) acquired, number of orders placed etc.
- Quality of acquisitions — Quality would include accuracy of order placement.
- Timeliness of acquisitions — This measure includes duration of time from order to receipt.

Operational function effectiveness measures

- See stock and equipment output measures.

Operational performance indicators

- Cost per title acquired
- Cost per item acquired
- Cost per order placed
- Average cost per accurately placed order.

Effectiveness indicators

- See effectiveness indicators for stock access and equipment access.

Cost-effectiveness indicators

- See cost-effectiveness indicators for stock access and equipment access.

Section 5. Methods for measuring input, output, effectiveness and domain values

5.1 Introduction

In this section we look at how to collect the measures listed in Section 2. The table below summarises examples of the methods for obtaining each measure.

Table 5.1

Measures	Methods
Service input costs	
• Amount of resources	Observe payments, record staff logs etc, cost finding for allocation of resources
Service output	
• Quantity of output	Staff records, library records, internal surveys
• Quality of output	Observation, internal surveys, peer review, expert review
• Timeliness of output	Staff records
• Availability	Library records
• Accessibility	Staff records, visitor survey, general user survey, specific service survey, population survey
Service effectiveness	
• Amount of use	Library records, visitor survey, general user survey, specific service survey, population survey
• Number of users	Library records, visitor survey, general user survey, specific service survey, population survey
• User perception of attributes	Visitor survey, general user survey, specific service survey, population survey
• User-expressed satisfaction	Visitor survey, general user survey, specific service survey, population survey
• User-indicated importance	Visitor survey, general user survey, specific service survey, population survey
• Purpose of use	Visitor survey, general user survey, specific service survey, population survey
• Consequences of use	Visitor survey, general user survey, specific service survey, population survey
• Number of persons in service population	Census records, local authority records
• Number of needs	Population survey, visitor survey, general user survey, specific service survey
• Number of needs filled	Population survey, visitor survey, general user survey, specific service survey

Some basic concepts of measures and methods are discussed in Appendix A. This section contains detailed discussions on measuring:

• staff costs

- costs of other resources
- output quantities and attributes
- service effectiveness and domain values.

5.2 Measuring staff costs

To measure staff costs associated with specific services we must know how much time is devoted to each service. Generally, the best method is to allocate staff time to appropriate services and operational functions.

Your results will be most accurate if you follow these rules and steps:

- Only allocate the time staff actually spend working at the library (that is, do not include holidays, sick leave etc).

- List all of the services or functions of interest. This list could include, for example, the 46 listed in Section 5.4 and discussed in Appendix A.

- Design an individual weekly time log (see Table 5.2 below).

- Design a worksheet for allocating individual staff time and salaries to services (see Table 5.3).

There are three ways to measure staff time:

- Use time sheets continuously or periodically throughout the year.

- Observe staff on a random basis to determine the proportion of time spent on specific activities, services or functions.

- Ask staff or their supervisors to estimate the proportion of time spent on specific activities, services or functions throughout a year.

Interestingly, the three ways of allocating staff time to services do not yield greatly different results.

Table 5.2 Example of a weekly time sheet
1) To be logged in 0.1 hour increments, for example, 0.2, 5.8, 5.5 etc.
2) A normal workday is 7.2 hours.

Service/function	Mon	Tues	Wed	Thurs	Fri	Sat/Sun	Total
1. Breaks	0.4 hrs	0.4 hrs	0.3 hrs	0.5 hrs	hrs	hrs	1.6 hrs
2. R&RA: directional	2.1	1.8	1.3	1.0			6.2
3. R&RA: reference	0.5	0.6	0.1	0.2			1.4
4. Issues	3.1	4.3	1.5	1.4			10.3
5. Shelving & reshelving				2.0			2.0
6. Photocopy services			4.0				4.0
7.							
8.							
9. Overhead	1.1	0.1		2.1			3.3
10. Other (specify)							
11. Holidays/sick leave					7.2		7.2
Total	7.2 hrs	7.2 hrs	7.2 hrs	7.2 hrs	7.2 hrs	hrs	36.0 hrs

	Day	Month		Day	Month	
Dates: Monday	_____	_____	to Sunday	_____	_____	1989

Employee signature _____

Supervisor signature _____

Table 5.3   Example of a staff allocation worksheet

Service/operational function	Hours 1,872	Hours (%)	Compensation £13,800	Hours 1,872	Hours (%)	Compensation £8,400	Total compensation £22,220
	Staff						
	A			**B**			
Stock development & management							
Acquisitions							
Post processing							
Cataloguing							
Catalogue maintenance							
Physical processing							
Periodicals binding							
Invoice processing							
Reference & readers advisory							
Directional	72	(3.8)	524	385	(20.6)	1,735	2,259
Reference	299	(16.0)	2,208	298	(15.9)	1,339	3,547
Online bibliographic searching							
Quick look-up	102	(5.4)	745				745
In-depth	391	(20.9)	2,884				2,884
Issues	87	(4.6)	635	521	(27.8)	2,341	2,976
Shelving & reshelving				104	(5.6)	471	471
Outreach services							
Activities							
Photocopy services				152	(8.1)	682	682
Equipment services							
Public relations							
Management & administration	431	(23.1)	3,188				3,188
Overhead & on costs	490	(26.2)	3,616	412	(22.0)	1,852	5,468

Using time sheets: an example

There are two staff members, A and B, involved in reference and readers advisory (R&RA) and online bibliographic searching (in addition to other services). The remaining services and functions and other staff are ignored for the purposes of the example.

Both staff members are asked to complete a weekly time sheet (see Table 5.2 for an example). Staff member A spends 1.6 hours on breaks, 6.2 hours on R&RA (directional enquiries) and so on. She also spends 3.3 hours on overhead activities (for example discussions, professional development etc) and 7.2 hours on sick leave. We can calculate the total hours she spends on specific services and functions in an entire year by adding the time logged on 52 weekly time sheets. In some instances the weekly time sheets can be kept for sampled periods and extrapolated to a full year.

The staff allocation worksheet (example given in Table 5.3) lists services and salaries for staff members A and B. The worksheets can be designed for all staff or subdivided by specific units or levels of staff depending on the size of the public library. The salaries can, and probably should, include any on-costs or other forms of compensation. The sample staff allocation worksheet records for each staff member the number of hours worked, the proportion of hours worked on specific services and the appropriate allocation of salaries.

For example, there are about 260 days or 1,872 work hours per year.

Staff member A has 42 days of sick leave and holidays, 5 days of professional development, about 2 days of breaks and about 19 days of other overhead time for a total of 68 days (490 hours) of overhead time. This overhead time can be recorded (as an indicator of efficiency) or it can be distributed across the other services and functions. The calculations below demonstrate both methods.

Total staff costs for services are calculated using the following steps:

- Calculate the proportion of hours devoted to each service by dividing the number of hours for each service by the total hours (for example 72 ÷ by 1,872 = 0.038 or 3.8%).

- The staff cost (for Staff member A) is calculated by multiplying the total compensation by the proportion of hours (for example £13,800 × 0.038 = £524).

- The total staff cost is found by adding the costs across staff members (for example £514 + £1,735 = £2,259).

The overhead and on-costs can be allocated across services as follows:

- Calculate the cost rate attributable to overhead and on-costs: £13,800 ÷ £13,800−£3,616 = £1,355 for Staff member A; and £8,400 ÷ £8,400−£1,852 = £1,283 for Staff member B.

- Multiply staff cost of each service by the relevant cost rate for each staff member (for example £524 × £1,355 = £710 for Staff member A; and £1,735 × £1,283 = £2,226 for Staff member B.

- Add new staff costs (for example £2,959 for directional R&RA).

Appropriate resource components should be identified for each activity and cost to be measured for resource components and staff activities. Suggestions are given below for recording these data, using an example. The sample spreadsheet format is at Table 5.4.

Table 5.4 Example of a spreadsheet for displaying input costs of services and functions

Service/function	Output quantities	Staff			Computer system/ equipment etc		External services	
		Staff member	Hours	£	Items	£	Items	£
Making photocopies	79,121 document copies	A	1,567	11,752	Photocopiers	8,809	None	
		B	462	3,615	Maintenance	656		
		C	108	934	Other	524		
Total	**732,758 pages**			**£16,301**		**£9,989**		

Facilities		Postage, envelopes, supplies etc		Collection		Other resources		Total
Items	£	Items	£	Items	£	Items	£	£
32m²	10,473	Paper	4,081	Allocation of collection use	30,400	None		
Furniture	58	Toner	326					
		Other	211					
Total	**£10,531**		**£4,618**		**£30,400**			**£71,839**

To determine staff time and costs we suggest that supervisors:

- establish about three to ten basic activities (see Appendix A for a list of 46 activities performed in many public libraries) for each staff member to be included on the time sheet. Use a combined log (that is, a log that combines input time and output quantities) if preferred. The activities given on the weekly time sheet are presented as examples. Items 2–9 could be left blank for supervisors to fill out for each staff member.

- determine which activities to record for each of their staff members. Generally, all of the 46 activities listed in Appendix A should be covered at minimum. Also include activities that involve substantial time or that the supervisor is interested in monitoring over time.

The amount of time devoted to various activities can be monitored over time to establish trends in the way in which staff members allocate their time, particularly for activities that do not deal directly with specific services (for example online bibliographic searching) or those related to specific output (for example number of items originally catalogued). Otherwise, the input time measures should be related to output measures to establish operational performance indicators.

Staff members should complete the weekly time sheet each day to the best of their abilities. Each day should include 7.2 hours for full-time staff. Time should be recorded to the nearest 0.1 hour to add up to 7.2 hours each day. Each week staff members should hand in a log that they have signed or initialled (at the bottom of the form). If absent, staff members should complete the logs on their return. Staff should also record the total amount of time for the week for each activity worked on during the week (that is, row totals). Staff costs will be determined by multiplying individual staff hours by staff rates (that is, salary plus on-costs divided by 1,872). You can do this easily if you have a computer spreadsheet program.

5.3 Measuring costs of other resources

Working out the cost of non-staff resources is more tricky. Often it is best to estimate cost of an activity item by item (for example total vendor invoices for online bibliographic searches; cost of photocopies etc for online searching). Other times the costs of some resources (for example computer system, postage, some supplies) can be established for services by allocating their total costs among service items. Such resource costs can be derived from line items in the library's budget.

Fixed costs may require depreciating expenditures over time. It may also be necessary to allocate the depreciated costs to activities. Depreciation involves spreading capital expenditures for such items as computer systems, microform reader/viewers, other equipment, facilities etc over a useful period of life (see Appendix A). If equipment and other similar expenditures have not been depreciated, the steps mentioned above provide a method for doing so.

Once a resource item's cost for a year is determined, it may be necessary to allocate the cost among two or more activities, since expenses for some resources or items might apply to more than one activity. Examples include depreciated computer system costs (for example £4,000 per year), annual fees, total postage costs etc. In these instances, the costs must be allocated between variable and fixed costs. Suggested steps for making such allocations are:

- Design an allocation worksheet (see example of other resource allocation worksheet in Table 5.5.

- For each resource, establish a reasonable basis for determining the proportion of costs that should be allocated to each service. For example, computer depreciation costs can be allocated on the basis of relative time used for services; postage can be allocated by number of items sent for the services etc.

- Allocate all computer time and, if idle time is known, the idle time can be allocated as well, depending on ability to determine proportion of time (see the previous section on allocation of staff overhead cost).

- Calculate and record the proportion of costs for each cost item.

- Estimate the costs of each service by multiplying the total costs by the proportion (for example 0.70 × £4,000 = £2,800 for computer).

- Find the total cost of other resources a service uses by adding together cost items for each service.

It makes sense to express costs in monetary units (£) to provide a common unit of input measurement for all resource and service costs.

A sample spreadsheet for displaying input costs (and output quantities) is given in Table 5.4. The example service on that spreadsheet is 'making photocopies'; resources used for the service include staff, photocopying equipment, facilities, supplies, and the stock. Stock costs are not normally allocated though they can be if so desired. The total cost of all resources for this service is £71,839. Cost per document photocopied is £0.90 per document copy and cost per page is £0.098 per page. Methods for measuring output quantities are discussed in the next subsection.

Table 5.5 Example of other resource allocation worksheet

| | | Cost item | | | | | | | | | |
| | Cost (£) | Computer | | Terminals | | Online vendors | | Annual fee | | Postage | |
		(%)	Cost (£)	(%)	Cost (£)	(%)	Cost (£)	(%)	Cost (£)	(%)	Cost (£)
Indirect costs											
Administration & management	10,400	(70)	2,800	(5)	400	(0)	0	(0)	0	(60)	7,200
Other	1,560	(5)	200	(2)	160	(0)	0	(0)	0	(10)	1,200
Computer system											
Computer	1,000	(25)	1,000	0	0	(0)	0	(0)	0	(0)	0
Service (direct) costs											
Online – variable	20,400	(0)	0	(0)	0	(100)	18,000	(0)	0	(20)	2,400
Online – fixed	4,000	(0)	0	(50)	4,000	(0)	0	(0)	0	(0)	0
Cataloguing – variable	600	(0)	0	0	0	(0)	0	(0)	0	(5)	600
Cataloguing – fixed	2,740	(0)	0	(23)	1,840	(0)	0	(60)	900	(0)	0
Interlibrary loan – variable	600	(0)	0	0	0	(0)	0	(0)	0	(5)	600
Interlibrary loan – fixed	2,200	(0)	0	(20)	1,600	(0)	0	(40)	600	(0)	0
Total costs	**43,500**	**(100)**	**4,000**	**(100)**	**8,000**	**(100)**	**18,000**	**(100)**	**1,500**	**(100)**	**12,000**

The costs of all resources are affected by the attributes of resources (for example the experience of staff, the storage capacity of computers).

The spreadsheet should record important attributes such as the staff level (that is, professional librarian, library technician, clerical support etc) and salary scale. In this way, staff productivity can be observed at several levels: individual staff productivity, productivity of each level of staff, productivity of all staff in the unit (department/group etc). It is not necessary to measure the attributes of other resource components on an ongoing basis unless current decisions regarding such attributes are to be made. If we decide to purchase new equipment, we can establish the effects of the various attributes of current computer systems, microcomputers, terminals, photocopiers, facilities etc on the service outputs (see Table 5.5).

5.4 Measuring service output quantities and attributes

For some activities, your library probably keeps (and certainly should keep) routine records of output quantities – issues, stock purchases, interlibrary loans, reference enquiries handled and so on. Attributes of output can be harder to measure, though often random spot checks or 100% observation by a supervisor or expert will be ways of checking quality, timeliness etc. Quality can be observed by supervisors (or someone else qualified to do so) through random inspection of the output of staff members' work.

Table 5.6 lists 19 basic services and 46 activities of a library together with suggestions for how to measure output quantities and attributes.

Output quantities

Output quantities can be measured by individual staff members. For example, a weekly output log can accompany the weekly time sheet for some activities. Table 5.7 is a sample of a weekly output log. On the log are output quantity measures and blank spaces for recording the amounts for each day of the week. Supervisors will have to determine which output quantities to collect in this manner and then record the appropriate output quantity measures on the form. The dates of data collection and signatures for both employees and supervisors should be obtained.

Staff who record their own output and the time they spend on an activity each day can find it eye-opening as they gain a sense of their own productivity.

Table 5.6 Output measures

	Quantities	Quality	Timeliness	Availability	Accessibility
Stock development and management					
1. Stock development	1) titles reviewed	NA	NA	NA	NA
	2) titles acquired	scope, comprehensiveness	NA	NA	NA
2. Stock weeding	titles withdrawn	requests after withdrawal	NA	NA	NA
Acquisitions					
3. Ordering	titles/items/subscriptions ordered	claims per order	order to receipt	item-days unavailable	NA
4. Processing stock received	items received	NA	throughput time	item-days unavailable	NA
5. Chasing	chases	NA	adherence to schedule	item-days unavailable	NA
6. Cancellations	titles cancelled	NA	NA	NA	NA
Post processing					
7. Post processing	1) packages processed	NA	throughput time	item-days unavailable	NA
	2) other items processed	NA	throughput time	item-days unavailable	NA
Cataloguing					
8. Copy and enhanced cataloguing	titles copy catalogued/ recatalogued & enhanced	% that conform to standards	throughput time	item-days unavailable	NA
9. Original cataloguing	titles originally catalogued	% that conform to standards	throughput time	item-days unavailable	NA
Catalogue maintenance					
10. Catalogue additions activities (cards)	titles catalogued (added)	accuracy of filing/ input	throughput time	item-days unavailable	NA
11. Catalogue withdrawal activities (cards)	titles withdrawn	NA	NA	NA	NA

Table 5.6 Output measures (continued)

	Quantities	Quality	Timeliness	Availability	Accessibility
Physical processing					
12. Spine labelling, barcode labelling/linking	1) items labelled 2) bound volumes returned	accuracy of labelling NA	throughput time throughput time	item-days unavailable item-days unavailable	NA NA
13. Other physical processing	items physically processed	quality of processing	throughput time	item-days unavailable	NA
14. Monograph binding and repair	items repaired	quality of repair	throughput time	item-days unavailable	NA
15. Acquisitions list	lists	NA	throughput time	NA	NA
Periodicals binding					
16. Preparing binding records	new journal titles (set-up)	accuracy of records	throughput time	NA	NA
17. Preparing materials to be bound	issues to be bound	NA	throughput time	article-days unavailable	NA
18. Processing returned bound volumes	returned bound volumes	quality of binding	throughput time	article-days unavailable	NA
Invoice processing					
19. Invoice processing	invoices processed	accuracy	throughput time	NA	NA
Reference and readers advisory (R&RA)					
20. Directional	directional requests	accuracy	NA	hours of service	waiting time
21. Reference	reference requests	relevance of response	1) speed of response 2) response from negotiated time	hours of service	waiting time
Online bibliographic searching					
22. Quick look-up	quick look-ups	accuracy of look-up	1) speed of response 2) response from negotiated time	hours of service	waiting time
23. In-depth	in-depth searches	1) relevance of response 2) number of items retrieved	1) speed of response 2) response from negotiated time	1) hours of service 2) person hours available	1) waiting time 2) number of host databases available
Issues					
24. Issues	items issued	NA	speed of response	1) hours of service 2) loan period 3) study seats/carrels	waiting time
Shelving and reshelving					
25. Shelving and reshelving	items shelved/reshelved	items shelved correctly	throughput time	item-days unavailable	NA

Table 5.6   Output measures (continued)

	Quantities	Quality	Timeliness	Availability	Accessibility
Interlibrary borrowing and lending					
26. Interlibrary borrowing	items borrowed	correct items processed	speed of response	NA	NA
27. Interlibrary lending	1) requests received	correct items processed	speed of response	NA	NA
	2) items loaned	correct items processed	speed of response	NA	NA
Outreach services					
28. Making contacts	contacts made	NA	NA	NA	NA
29. Performing services	number of services	quality	NA	NA	NA
Activities					
30. Preparing for activities	number of services	NA	NA	NA	NA
31. Conducting activities	number of services	quality	NA	NA	NA
Photocopy services					
32. Making photocopies	pages photocopied	NA	throughput time	NA	NA
33. Providing pay photocopy machines	pages photocopied	NA	throughput time	NA	NA
34. Providing maintenance and supply	days open & closed	NA	late opening	NA	NA
Equipment services					
35. Providing instruction	number of services	NA	NA	NA	NA
36. Maintenance and upkeep	number of services	NA	NA	NA	NA
Public relations					
37. Preparing exhibits and promotional materials	exhibits & material prepared	quality of exhibits	time from schedule	NA	NA
38. Conducting tours and/or present briefings	tours and/or briefings	quality of tours/ briefings	time from schedule	NA	NA
Management and administration					
39. General administration	NA	NA	NA	NA	NA
40. Secretarial/clerical related activities	NA	NA	NA	NA	NA
41. Statistical and financial management	NA	NA	NA	NA	NA
42. Personnel management and staff development	NA	NA	NA	NA	NA
43. Computer, equipment and systems related activities	NA	NA	NA	NA	NA
44. Facilities management	NA	NA	NA	NA	NA
45. Contract services	NA	NA	NA	NA	NA
46. Marketing, public relations etc	NA	NA	NA	NA	NA

Table 5.7 Sample weekly output log

1) Record amount of output each day – completed work only

Output quantity measures	Mon	Tues	Wed	Thurs	Fri	Sat/ Sun	Total
1. R&RA: directional							
2. R&RA: reference							
3. Issues							
4. Shelving & reshelving							
5. Photocopy services							
6. _____							
7. _____							
8. _____							
9. _____							
10. _____							
11. _____							
Total							

	Day	Month		Day	Month	
Dates: Monday	_____	_____	to Sunday	_____	_____	1989

Employee signature _____

Supervisor signature _____

Service output attributes

Service output attributes include quality, timeliness, availability and accessibility of services and operational functions. These are generally more difficult to measure than service output quantities. Five methods can be used to measure service output attributes:

1) Observation of all output

- Quality of services can be measured by observing all output and determining quality. This means that every item, unit or transaction must be observed over a specified period of time. The observation of quality can be made by a supervisor, panel of peers or someone who is independent of the public library.

- Timeliness is determined by recording when events take place. Standards for the timeliness of an activity can be based on a proportion of events that are to be accomplished within a specified period of time. Acceptable performance might be that no events take longer than a specified time to accomplish. All events (100%) should be observed to make sure that acceptable standards of timeliness are achieved.

2) Random sampling of output

- In many instances, it is difficult or expensive to observe the quality of all instances of output. In these instances, the output should be sampled and inspected for timeliness or quality.

3) Random spot checks

- Spot checks determine whether or not activities are being performed as specified. This method is useful for observing availability. For example, the issue desk might be observed at random times to ensure that it is staffed, that long queues have not formed, and that users are being served promptly and courteously. Spot checks performed weekly or monthly can verify that this is happening.

4) User feedback including user surveys

- A survey of users may be conducted to determine whether performance standards are being met (for example that standards for timeliness and quality of reference services are maintained from the user perspective).

5) Verified user complaints

- User complaints should be encouraged, received and verified to ensure the quality and timeliness of work performed. All complaints should be responded to and the causes of the problems determined and addressed.

Each of these methods is described in more detail below and examples are given in the next section.

To observe timeliness by checking all output, we must maintain records of transactions. As an example, a log can be maintained for each order recording the date of request, date of order placement, date of return, date of delivery, and so on. The logs (maintained manually or on an automated system) can highlight activities that deviate from performance standards of timeliness. In other instances, the timeliness of activities, such as delivery of periodic reports, can be observed through a review of each report and its delivery.

The second principal method of measurement is random sampling. In this case, a periodic (usually quarterly) lot or batch of output is sampled and inspected. A supervisor, or someone designated by the supervisor, should determine whether sample outputs conform to library standards. For example, assume that there are approximately 600 items catalogued annually at the library. These 600 items are subdivided into quarterly output and are randomly sampled using the following methods. About 150 items are originally catalogued quarterly. These are the lots to be sampled.

There are two ways in which random samples may be selected.

1) Random number tables

- List a lot (or batch) from which the sample will be drawn.

- Identify each item uniquely with a number (1 to the number of items in the lot).

- Choose random numbers from a table of numbers and assign numbers to the items in the lot. This represents the sample.

2) Systematic random sampling

- In this procedure, divide the lot size (that is, number of items in the lot) by the sample size to determine a sampling interval (for example every 10th of 32nd record). Determine the first sample item by choosing a random number from one to the number in the sample interval (for example 10 or 32) using the table of random numbers. Choose the remaining sampled items systematically by counting the interval (the 10th or 32nd item after the first item sampled). For example, if the sampling interval is 32 and the first random number is 24, the samples are 24, 56, 88, 120, 152 etc.

Sometimes activities or events must be observed visually. For instance, are staff available to provide a service? A supervisor or manager should make random spot checks on the operation. Such spot checks should be weekly or monthly depending on the observation made. Spot checking means that staff will know that certain activities have to be performed and performed on time.

5.5 Measuring service effectiveness and domain values

To measure effectiveness and domain values you must conduct surveys: surveys of the population served as a whole, and surveys of users and visitors. As surveys are both costly and time consuming it is important to be clear about what information you will gather from the survey, and how to gather it, as well as how to interpret it afterwards. Here we examine types of surveys and questionnaires.

Types of surveys

There are four types of surveys that can be used to measure effectiveness indicators:

- General population survey – Encompasses all people in the geographic area served by a public library. It allows you to measure factors that affect library use which cannot be measured from library users alone. These measures include:

  - awareness of the library and of specific services;
  - distance to the library;
  - special factors that affect use (for example physical disabilities, literacy)
  - population attributes.

  These measures (except awareness) can be obtained by comparing user data with existing statistics (assuming they are available). You should conduct this kind of survey once every several years (for example once every five years).

- General user survey – This survey is performed by sampling a list of users, for example, a list of registered borrowers. The principal purpose is to measure:

  - the extent to which the library and specific services are used;
  - awareness of specific services;
  - general importance of and satisfaction with public library resources and services;
  - distance to the library;
  - user attributes.

  This survey should be conducted about every other year.

- Visitor survey – This survey is of visitors to a public library. It provides general measures of:
  - frequency of use of the library and of specific services;
  - importance of and satisfaction with resources and services;
  - distance to the library;
  - user attributes.

  This survey should be conducted periodically over time (for example quarterly) and analysed once a year.

  The visitor survey is the most fundamental survey for public libraries. It is also the easiest to administer. There are three steps:

  - design and test a questionnaire;
  - establish a sampling scheme by which sampled visitors can be handed questionnaires to be filled out in the library or posted to the library (or returned on a later visit) if the visitor cannot complete it on site;
  - maintain accurate data on total number of visitors during the time the survey is being conducted (for example a week). This information is important for estimating total annual visits and number of users.

- Specific service survey – Suppose that we have reason to be concerned about a specific service, such as reference and information. This survey analyses in depth specific services such as reference and information services, interlibrary borrowing (for users) and lending (borrowing library as a user), services to special groups, and activities.

  The survey should be conducted with recent users of the specific services and should emphasise:

  - frequency of use of the service;

– importance and satisfaction with detailed attributes of resources and output measures of service (all for a specific incident of use such as most recent use);
– purpose of use;
– consequences of use;
– user attributes.

Such surveys should be conducted periodically, about every other year. Some of these specific service surveys can also be performed quarterly, if you suspect that measures vary seasonally.

These four kinds of surveys provide all of the effectiveness measures needed for deriving many of the effectiveness indicators, cost-effectiveness indicators and impact indicators. Yet each type of survey is done only periodically (albeit with differing frequencies) and with a limited amount of data collection to minimise the burden on respondents (and on library staff for processing and analysis).

Brief questionnaires also help ensure sufficient response rates. Survey tests suggest that high response rates (over 75%) can be expected by libraries. Appendix A presents a thorough discussion of data collection methods, questionnaire design, sample design and data processing.

Survey questionnaire items

This subsection presents some examples of questions that can be used on questionnaires for any of the four types of surveys. In particular the examples include questions dealing with public library service: (1) frequency of visits and use; (2) performance, satisfaction and importance; (3) purpose of use; (4) awareness of services; and (5) user demographics. Note that number of visits and use are often related to the other measures. Some further concepts and detailed discussion related to questionnaire design are provided in Appendix A.

Frequency of visits and use

One measure of frequency of use is the number of visits to the public library. There are several ways that one can measure number of visits as shown below.

● **Approximately how many times have you visited the BLANK public library in the past year (that is, 12 months)?**

---------- times last year

Recall of events can be a problem with this form of the question. Furthermore, if there are seasonal effects, the annual estimates may be biased unless this question is asked several times over the year. Respondents sometimes have a tendency to answer for one month rather than one year.

● **How many times have you visited the BLANK public library in the past year (that is, 12 months)? (CIRCLE ONE.)**

1–5 times 1

6–10 times 2

11–15 times 3

16–20 times 4

More than 20 times (please specify how many) 5

---------- times

OR

- **How often do you usually visit the BLANK public library? (CIRCLE ONE.)**

  This is my first visit 1

  Less than once a year 2

  Once a year 3

  Several times a year 4

  Once a month 5

  Once a week or more 6

These methods of asking about frequency of use of the library have the advantage of taking seasonal effects into account. However, the responses must be 'improvised' to make estimates of total visits (for example, 0.5 for 'less than once a year'; 6 for 'several times a year'; 125 for 'twice a week or more'). Formal methods of improvising are discussed in Appendix A. These methods have been shown to provide annual estimates that are reasonably accurate, but not very precise.

- **When did you last visit the public library?**

  ------------------------- month ---------------- year

This method has the advantage of being simpler to answer and requires less recall on the part of the user. However, the calculation of total number of visits is not simple. The question provides a rough estimate of the duration of time between visits (that is, current time minus number of months ago). If, for example, it has been three months, we divide 12 months by 3 to provide an estimate of 4 visits per year. The method provides neither precise nor accurate estimates.

The amount of use of specific library services can be measured in two ways. The first is to count visits to the library and establish the proportion of visits during which a specific service is used (for example asked librarian for help in finding information, used the catalogue, used the photocopier) or the number of uses of a service per visit (for example number of reference books looked at, number of pages photocopied). The proportion of visits during which a service is used can be estimated from the following type of question:

- **What did you do on your visit to the library today? (CIRCLE ALL THAT APPLY.)**

  Looked for a specific book, magazine, record etc .... a

  Browsed for reading materials .... b

  Used the catalogue to identify and locate materials c

  Consulted books or magazines for specific information .... d

  Asked librarian for help in finding information .... e

  Collected information asked for earlier .... f

  Read books, magazines or newspapers .... g

  Studied in library with own material .... h

  Used photocopier i

  Other (please specify) --- j

This question is used in a visitor survey. For a general user survey, we ask questions about the most recent visit (that is, a critical incidence) in the following manner:

- **What did you do on your last visit to the library?** (CIRCLE ALL THAT APPLY.)

If there is likely to be more than a single use on a visit one can either isolate that service or inject it in answers to the question above:

- Read books, magazines or newspapers .... g

  If you read books, magazines or newspapers, how many of them did you read?

  .... books

  .... magazines

  .... newspapers

- Used photocopier i

  If you used photocopier, how many articles (or pages) were photocopied?

  .... articles or .... pages

Another general method is simply to ask how many times a service has been used in the last month:

- How many times in the last month have you asked a librarian for help in finding information?

  .... times in the last month

- How many times in the last month have you read books, magazines or newspapers in the library?

  .... times in the last month

Performance, satisfaction and importance

Performance, satisfaction and importance are all difficult concepts to measure. They should be measured for both services and resources in general, as well as for specific attributes of the services and resources. One useful way to measure performance, satisfaction and importance is to use rating scales. There is a controversy in the survey field concerning whether rating scales should include an even number of points (for example 1, 2, 3, 4) or an odd number (for example 1, 2, 3, 4, 5). Examples below all use a rating scale of 1 to 5. Rating scales can be presented as questions concerning services as follows:

- **How do you rate reference services in the BLANK public library?** (CIRCLE APPROPRIATE NUMBER.)

Very bad	Bad	Neither good nor bad	Good	Very good
1	2	3	4	5

- **How satisfied are you with reference services in the BLANK public library?** (CIRCLE APPROPRIATE NUMBER.)

Very dissatisfied	Dissatisfied	Neither satisfied nor dissatisfied	Satisfied	Very satisfied
1	2	3	4	5

- **How important to you are the reference services of the BLANK public library? (CIRCLE APPROPRIATE NUMBER.)**

Very unimportant	Unimportant	Neither important nor unimportant	Important	Very important
1	2	3	4	5

For some services it may be best to ask about service attributes such as quality, timeliness, availability, accessibility etc. When this is done a specific incident of use should be identified and questions asked about that use. For example:

- **Please answer all questions below for the last reference search performed for you by BLANK public library.**

- **How long did it take the reference librarian to respond to your reference request?**

    .... hours or .... days

- **How do you rate the response time of this last reference request? (CIRCLE APPROPRIATE NUMBER)**

Very bad	Bad	Neither good nor bad	Good	Very good
1	2	3	4	5

- **How satisfied are you with the response time of this last reference request?**

Very dissatisfied	Dissatisfied	Neither satisfied nor dissatisfied	Satisfied	Very satisfied
1	2	3	4	5

- **How important is response time to this last reference report?**

Very unimportant	Unimportant	Neither important nor unimportant	Important	Very important
1	2	3	4	5

Ratings of performance and satisfaction tend to be very similar. Satisfaction appears easier for users to answer than performance ratings. It is useful to measure both satisfaction and importance because there is different interpretation if a person is dissatisfied with the service (attribute) depending on whether the service is important or not to the user.

One can compare performance, satisfaction and importance across services (and attributes) by comparing average ratings (from 1 to 5 in the above examples). Another comparison can be made by ranking services or levels of attributes. For example one can ask library users to rank services:

- **Please rank the following four services in order of importance (satisfaction of performance) to you, where 1 is most important and 4 is least important. (WRITE IN THE RANK FOR EACH SERVICE – 1 to 4.)**

	Rank
Stock of books and other materials	-------
Catalogue in the library	-------
Reference services	-------
Photocopy service	-------

One problem with ranking is that it is difficult to establish the relative importance of the items ranked. For example, users may consider stock not only to be most important, but far more important than the service ranked second. There is no way to tell this. An example in Section 6.4 presents a very powerful (but difficult to implement) method called conjoint measurement for determining the relative importance of service attributes. More discussion of rating and ranking can be found in Appendix A.

More about satisfaction ratings

What we have learned so far about satisfaction ratings generally applies to performance and importance ratings as well. Satisfaction ratings can be used to assess public library resources or services. It is important to be clear about the attributes or output measures of interest. Also, it is often useful to clarify why respondents are dissatisfied if they so indicate. We recommend a rating scale of 1 to 5 because descriptions can easily be given to five levels as follows:

Very dissatisfied	Dissatisfied	Neither satisfied nor dissatisfied	Satisfied	Very satisfied
1	2	3	4	5

Note that the scale from low to high is correlated with level of satisfaction. That is, higher ratings reflect greater satisfaction. Sometimes respondents reverse the scale in their minds. If they are asked to clarify why they are dissatisfied, this reversal will become apparent and can be corrected during questionnaire editing. Further, it is useful to have an NA (that is, not applicable) response for those who do not use a service; otherwise respondents tend to circle number 3 – 'Neither satisfied nor dissatisfied'.

'Satisfaction' questions

Examples of satisfaction questions concerning library resources are:

- **How satisfied are you with the stock of books, magazines etc that this public library has? (CIRCLE APPROPRIATE NUMBER. CIRCLE NA IF YOU HAVE NOT USED THE STOCK.)**

Very dissatisfied	Dissatisfied	Neither satisfied nor dissatisfied	Satisfied	Very satisfied	Not applicable
1	2	3	4	5	NA

If you are very dissatisfied or dissatisfied, please indicate why.

- **How satisfied are you with the helpfulness of library staff?** (CIRCLE APPROPRIATE NUMBER.)

Very dissatisfied	Dissatisfied	Neither satisfied nor dissatisfied	Satisfied	Very satisfied
1	2	3	4	5

If you are very dissatisfied or dissatisfied, please indicate why.

- **How satisfied are you with the library facilities such as the building, the layout, seating etc?** (CIRCLE APPROPRIATE NUMBER.)

Very dissatisfied	Dissatisfied	Neither satisfied nor dissatisfied	Satisfied	Very satisfied
1	2	3	4	5

If you are very dissatisfied or dissatisfied, please indicate why.

- **How satisfied are you with the location of the library in your community?** (CIRCLE APPROPRIATE NUMBER.)

Very dissatisfied	Dissatisfied	Neither satisfied nor dissatisfied	Satisfied	Very satisfied
1	2	3	4	5

If you are very dissatisfied or dissatisfied, please indicate why.

- **How satisfied are you with the hours during which the library is open?** (CIRCLE APPROPRIATE NUMBER.)

Very dissatisfied	Dissatisfied	Neither satisfied nor dissatisfied	Satisfied	Very satisfied
1	2	3	4	5

If you are very dissatisfied or dissatisfied, please indicate why.

Examples of questions concerning satisfaction with reference resources and services are:

- **How satisfied are you with the ability of the reference library staff to help you locate needed information and materials?** (CIRCLE APPROPRIATE NUMBER. IF YOU DO NOT USE REFERENCE STAFF CIRCLE NA FOR NOT APPLICABLE.)

Very dissatisfied	Dissatisfied	Neither satisfied nor dissatisfied	Satisfied	Very satisfied	Not applicable
1	2	3	4	5	NA

If you are very dissatisfied or dissatisfied, please indicate why.

- **How satisfied are you with the approachability and responsiveness of reference library staff?** (CIRCLE APPROPRIATE NUMBER. IF YOU DO NOT USE REFERENCE STAFF CIRCLE NA FOR NOT APPLICABLE.)

Very dissatisfied	Dissatisfied	Neither satisfied nor dissatisfied	Satisfied	Very satisfied	Not applicable
1	2	3	4	5	NA

If you are very dissatisfied or dissatisfied, please indicate why.

- **How satisfied are you with the content of the reference library's collection of books, magazines etc?** (CIRCLE APPROPRIATE NUMBER.)

Very dissatisfied	Dissatisfied	Neither satisfied nor dissatisfied	Satisfied	Very satisfied	Not applicable
1	2	3	4	5	NA

If you are very dissatisfied or dissatisfied, please indicate why.

- **How satisfied are you with the general facilities provided in the reference library (general layout, seating arrangements etc)?** (CIRCLE APPROPRIATE NUMBER.)

Very dissatisfied	Dissatisfied	Neither satisfied nor dissatisfied	Satisfied	Very satisfied	Not applicable
1	2	3	4	5	NA

If you are very dissatisfied or dissatisfied, please indicate why.

Examples of questions concerning satisfaction with services to housebound readers are:

- **How satisfied are you with the service in general?** (CIRCLE APPROPRIATE NUMBER.)

Very dissatisfied	Dissatisfied	Neither satisfied nor dissatisfied	Satisfied	Very satisfied	Not applicable
1	2	3	4	5	NA

If you are very dissatisfied or dissatisfied, please indicate why.

- **How satisfied are you with the frequency of visits?** (CIRCLE APPROPRIATE NUMBER.)

Very dissatisfied	Dissatisfied	Neither satisfied nor dissatisfied	Satisfied	Very satisfied	Not applicable
1	2	3	4	5	NA

If you are very dissatisfied or dissatisfied, please indicate why.

- **How satisfied are you with the reading materials you get?** (CIRCLE APPROPRIATE NUMBER.)

Very dissatisfied	Dissatisfied	Neither satisfied nor dissatisfied	Satisfied	Very satisfied	Not applicable
1	2	3	4	5	NA

If you are very dissatisfied or dissatisfied, please indicate why.

- **How satisfied are you with the helpfulness of the library staff who visit you?** (CIRCLE APPROPRIATE NUMBER.)

Very dissatisfied	Dissatisfied	Neither satisfied nor dissatisfied	Satisfied	Very satisfied	Not applicable
1	2	3	4	5	NA

If you are very dissatisfied or dissatisfied, please indicate why.

Note that the process of estimating the total number of visits or uses of specific services is particularly difficult for visitor surveys. These difficulties are discussed under calculation methods and analysis in Section 6.2 and in Appendix A.3.1.1.

Purpose of use

Purpose of use can be measured by asking users the purpose associated with a particular use of a service or in visiting the library in general. Examples are as follows:

- **For what purpose did you need the information/materials sought in the library?** (CIRCLE ALL THAT APPLY.)

  Work-related .... a

  School or college .... b

  Hobby c

  General recreation .... d

  Travel .... e

  Other (please specify) -- f

The question above addresses general purposes of using reference services. Another, more specific set of purposes of use involves library services to the housebound as follows:

- **What information would you like the librarian to find for you?** (CIRCLE ALL THAT APPLY.)

  Neighbourhood/community .... a

  Consumer (for example shopping, complaints) .... b

  Housing/home care c

  Work .... d

  Education .... e

  Health .... f

  Transportation .... g

  Recreation .... h

  Holiday and holiday accommodation i

  Money matters .... j

  Child care .... k

  Other family relations l

  Legal matters .... m

  Crime and safety .... n

  Current events and news .... o

  Other (please specify) -- p

Awareness of services

Use of library services is often affected by awareness of the services. Awareness can be measured by the proportion of users who are aware of the service:

- **Even though you may not frequently use a public library, there may be services that you would use if you were aware of them. The following is a list of some services provided by the BLANK public library. Please circle a '1' if you are not aware of the service and would never use it; a '2' if you are not aware of the service, but might use it; and a '3' if you are not aware and will use it; a '4' if you are aware of the service but never used it; or a '5' if you are aware and do use the service.**

Table 5.8

	Not aware			Aware	
	Would never use	Now aware, might use	Now aware, will use	But never used	Do use
a. Assistance from a library staff person in identifying or locating relevant materials	1	2	3	4	5
b. Telephone reference/information service	1	2	3	4	5
c. Catalogue of library's collection..	1	2	3	4	5

The range of possible responses given in Table 5.8 provides not only a method for estimating the proportion of users who are aware of a service, but also the proportion that might use the service once they become aware of it. Awareness questions are particularly important in a general population survey, because it is the only survey in which one can measure the extent to which the population is aware of the public library and of its services.

User demographics

Several population or user characteristics are known to relate to the extent of use of public libraries. These characteristics include: distance to library (although this measure might be thought of an accessibility measure), age, sex, education and occupation.

Distance to the library can be measured in a number of ways, although it is important to distinguish between how far one lives from the library (general population and user surveys) and how far one came to make a specific visit to the library (visitor survey), because a user may visit while on a shopping trip, on the way to or from work etc. Two ways to ask distance are:

● **How far did you come to visit the library today? (PLEASE ESTIMATE AS BEST YOU CAN.)**

   ------- miles

● **How long did it take you to get to the library on this visit?**

   ------- minutes

Asking the question in terms of the user's time is generally preferable because it is easier to answer. Furthermore, time is an indicator of value of the library to users, because users 'pay' to use the library in terms of their time. It is also useful to have some information on how the visitor travelled to the library (for example walked, bus, car) and from where they left to visit the library (for example home, work, school, college, shops).

The remaining demographic characteristics can be asked in a general question:

- **Please answer the following questions which will be used to analyse the information provided by all those filling in questionnaires. (CIRCLE APPROPRIATE RESPONSE.)**

Age:

Under 18 1
18–24 2
25–44 3
45–64 4
65 or over 5

Sex:

Male 1
Female 2

Education (highest level achieved):

Secondary 1
Further education 2
University 3

Occupation ---

Occupation can be open-ended, but it is somewhat difficult to classify responses.

Open-ended question at the end of questionnaire

There is substantial merit in leaving space for additional comments by respondents at the very end of the questionnaire. Many respondents will not comment; however, some may wish to do so and will be unhappy if they are not given a formal opportunity to do so. Often such comments are very valuable and provide useful insights. An example of this type of question is:

- **Do you have any further comments or suggestions about the BLANK public library?**

109

Section 6. Methods for calculating measures and derived indicators

6.1 Why use statistical methods?

The statistical methods to calculate measures and derived indicators are simple but essential. As statistical methods are used to gather data, we must use the right statistical procedures to analyse those data.

In this section we work through how to calculate means, proportions and totals, depending on how we designed our sample. We present examples of how to calculate estimates of the number of:

● visits and users;

● uses of specific services;

● satisfaction with services and their attributes.

Appendix A.3.1.3 explains how to calculate the confidence limits of our measurements – that is, how large a margin of error is built into our samples.

Your library or branch library may not have the computer hardware and software for statistical estimations and tabulations. We therefore demonstrate how the data can be manipulated by hand.

Once we have collected data and measured the factors that interest us, we can derive indicators from the measures. The last part of this section explains how.

6.2 Number of users and visits to the library

In some instances public libraries have accurate measures of the number of current users (from up-to-date registration files) and library visits (from gate counts or people counters). Often, though, either:

- the registration file does not reflect changes in user status (that is, moved, deceased or simply no longer using the library); or

- the method of keeping gate counts (people counters) is not implemented or is inaccurate.

In these circumstances measures can be obtained by survey — either general user (or population) survey or a visitor survey.

General user and population surveys

General user and population surveys are less likely to be used than visitor surveys. However, they both provide simple estimates of the number of visits and service uses. It is necessary only to ask how many times respondents visit (or use) the public library. Responses can be either a number of times or a circled range of number of visits (see examples under 'Visitor surveys' below). If users tend to visit the library a great deal (for example over 50 times per year) it may be best to ask them how often they visit the library each month. However, few public libraries have average visits that high, and number of visits over a year is a valid time period.

To calculate:

- average number of visits — add up all the responses and divide by the total number of responses;

- total number of visits — multiply the average number of visits by the total number of library users.

In a general user survey, you should know the total number of users before you begin, because you will use a listing of users to select your survey sample.

In a population survey, derive the number of users by first estimating the proportion of the population that uses the public library and multiply this by the total number of people in the population.

Visitor surveys

It is more difficult to estimate both number of visits and number of users through visitor surveys, although the survey itself is generally simpler to administer and is less expensive than general user and population surveys.

Visitor surveys must be stratified by number of visits per year (or month) because sample selection is based on visits and not users. Thus, frequent visitors (users) have a greater chance of being sampled than infrequent visitors, and unless our calculations allow for this the results will be biased.

As described in Section 5, number of visits can be asked on the visitor questionnaires in several ways:

- **How many times have you visited this public library in the past year (that is, 12 months)?**
  -------- times last year

- **How many times have you visited this public library in the past year (that is, 12 months)? (CIRCLE AS APPROPRIATE.)**

  1–5 times 1

  6–10 times 2

  11–15 times 3

  16–20 times 4

  More than 20 times (specify how many) 5

  -------- times

- **How often do you (or would you if new to the area) visit this public library? (CIRCLE ONE.)**

  Less than once a year 1
  Once a year 2
  Several times a year 3
  Once a month 4
  Twice a month 5
  Once a week 6
  Twice a week or more (specify approximately how many times a week) 7
  .... times/week

To estimate total and average visits or total users it is necessary to post-stratify by number of visits. An example is given below (Croydon Information Centre) for the second method of asking number of visits.

Croydon sampled visits over a one-week period (10 October 1988 to 17 October 1988). They counted a total of 3,622 visits during this period. They sampled 207 visits during this time and 158 complete and usable questionnaires were received (for a very respectable 76% response rate).* A total of 152 visitors answered the number of visits question as seen in Table 6.1.

Table 6.1

Number of visits	Number of visitors	Estimated total number of visits	Estimated average number of visits	Estimated total number of users
1–5	70	86,730	2.2	39,423
6–10	30	37,170	7.7	4,827
11–15	16	19,824	12.8	1,549
16–20	8	9,912	17.9	554
More than 20	28	34,692	44.7	776
Total	**152**	**188,328**	**4.0**	**47,129**

Of the 152 visitors sampled, 70 visitors said they visited 1 to 5 times, 30 said they visited 6 to 10 times etc.

Below we work through the steps by which Croydon calculated the data in Table 6.1.

To calculate the total number of visits to the library over a full year, multiply 3,622 visits in the sampled week by 52 weeks:

Estimated total number of visits = $3,622 \times 52 = 188,344$

To calculate the weighting to be attached to each respondent, divide the estimated total number of visits for the year by the number of visitors sampled:

$$\text{Weight} = \frac{\text{Total number of visits for the year}}{\text{Number of respondents}}$$

$$\text{Weight} = \frac{188,344}{152} = 1,239$$

To calculate the total number of visits made by people from each stratum (for example those visiting the library 1–5 times per year), multiply the number of respondents in the group by the weighting:

Total number of visits made by people visiting the library 1–5 times per year = 70 (number of respondents) × 1,239 (weighting) = 86,730

(For those visiting 6–10 times, the calculation is 30 × 1,239 = 37,170.)

---

* Actually the days were sub-divided into three time periods: 9.30–13.00; 13.00–16.00 and 16.00 to close of the day (19.00 on Monday and 18.00 on other days) and 9.30–13.00 and 13.00–17.00 on Saturday. This stratification is ignored in order to simplify the example above.

To calculate the estimated average number of visits per person in each stratum, find the geometric average of the number of visits range. This is the square root of the product of the numbers at the top and bottom of the range:

$$\text{Average number of visits per person} = \sqrt{1 \times 5} = 2.2$$
$$= \sqrt{6 \times 10} = 7.7$$

Because there is no range given over 20, the geometric average is calculated by plotting the points for the lower ranges on a graph (see Figure 6.2) and extrapolating. This method is quite acceptable where the data distribution is log-normal – that is, it falls in a straight line on a log-normal probability chart. When the line is extrapolated to 98%, there are approximately 100 visits per year; therefore calculating for the range 20 to 100:

$$\text{Average number of visits per person} = \sqrt{20 \times 100} = 44.7$$

Note that the sum of the number of visits on Table 6.1 is 188,328 and not 188,344 as initially calculated due to rounding of the weight (1.239).

To calculate the total number of users in each stratum of frequency of visits, divide the estimated total number of visits per year by the average number of visits per person per year:

$$\text{Total number of users} = \frac{\text{Estimated total number of visits}}{\text{Estimated average number of visits}}$$
$$= \frac{86,730}{2.2} = 39,423$$

When this has been done for each stratum, sum the total number of users in each stratum to obtain the total number of users of the library as a whole for one year: 47,129.

A less formal way of asking number of visits was given above with responses such as 'less than once a year', 'once a year', 'several times a year' etc. Most of these responses imply an average rather than a range. Thus, once a year would be counted as 1; once a month as 12; twice a month as 24 etc. Several times a year would have an estimated average of 4.6 (that is $\sqrt{2 \times 11}$ assuming log-normality). Estimated total visits and total users are calculated in much the same manner as above (see Figure 6.1).

Estimating the total number of users for each class of frequency of visits (that is, stratum) is essential because one must use these numbers to weight the responses to each question that is relevant to users. Some questions on the visitor survey questionnaire will be relevant to visits and some will be relevant to users. For example, typical questions related to visits and users are as follows:

Visit-related questions

- What did you do on your visit to the public library today?

- Did you ask the staff for help in finding the information and/or materials you were looking for?

- For what purpose did you need the information/materials sought in the public library?

- Approximately when did you arrive at (or leave) the public library today?

User-related questions

- How satisfied are you with the ability of the public library staff to help you locate needed information and materials?

- How satisfied are you with the public library's stock of books and other materials?

- How old are you?

Figure 6.1

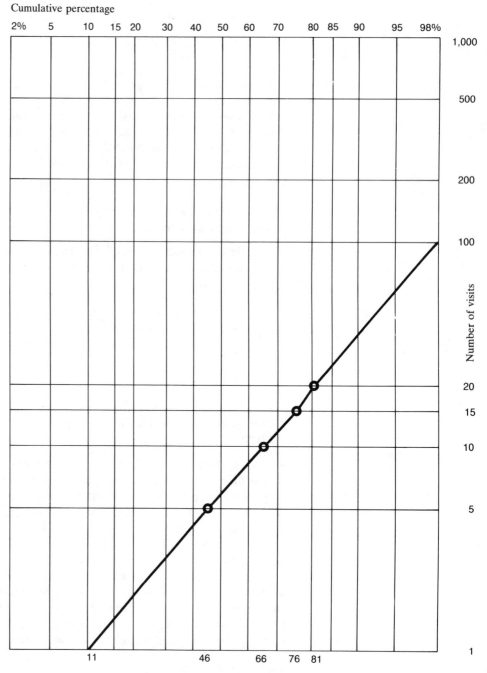

Some questions can be relevant to either visit or user depending on how the question was asked. For example:

- 'How long does it normally take you to get to the public library?' is user-related.

- 'How long did it take you to get to the public library on this visit?' is visit-related.

As indicated above, calculating measures from user-related questions is not straightforward when data are taken from a visitor survey. To demonstrate this, an example is given below for estimating the proportions of users who are male and female, and number of visits by each. In this example (again from Croydon) there were 156 visitors who responded to the question concerning their sex.

Table 6.2

Number of visits	Male Sample	Male Sample proportion (%)	Male Population total	Female Sample	Female Sample proportion (%)	Female Population total	Both Sample	Both Population total
1–5	29	(40.8)	16,085	42	(59.2)	23,338	71	39,423
6–10	18	(58.1)	2,804	13	(41.9)	2,023	31	4,827
11–15	11	(64.7)	1,002	6	(35.3)	547	17	1,549
16–20	8	(100.0)	554	0	(0)	0	8	554
More than 20	25	(86.2)	669	4	(13.8)	107	29	776
Total	**91**	**(58.3)**	**21,114**	**65**	**(41.7)**	**26,015**	**156**	**47,129**

Without weighting, we would assume from the sample that 58.3% of the users are male (that is, 91 ÷ 156 = 0.583). However, weighting by number of users in each stratum yields a very different result. Estimates in each stratum are calculated by taking the proportion of males and females in each stratum and multiplying them by the number of users in the stratum.

For example, the number of males in the stratum of those who visit 1 to 5 times per year is estimated to be 16,085 (that is, 0.408 times 39,423) and the number of females is 23,338 (that is, 0.592 times 39,423). Considering all classes of number of visits, we find that the weighted estimate of proportion of users who are male is 44.8% (that is, 21,114 divided by 47,129) compared with the 58.3% calculated from unweighted data. Actually, 58.3% is the proportion of visits that are by males. In this example the reason that the weighted results are so different from unweighted results is that infrequent visits tend to be made more by females and frequent visits by males, and there are many more users who are infrequent visitors than frequent visitors.

The average numbers of visits by males and females are 5.2 visits per person for males and 3.0 visits per person for females. These averages are calculated by multiplying average number of visits in each stratum times the total persons (for example 2.2 times 16,085), summing over the five strata and dividing by the total number in the population of interest (for example, 21,114 males). Note that the unweighted estimates would be 17.6 and 6.9 visits per person respectively, for males and females. Thus, the weighted estimates substantially affect estimates of proportions and averages, as well as totals.

Amount of use of specific services can be measured using the visitor survey or a survey of the service itself. Use the latter when you need substantial information about a particular service. There are two general approaches to estimating the amount of use:

(1) Determine whether or not a service is used during a particular visit and project the result to number of visits.

(2) Ask users to indicate the number of times they use a particular service (in a month if use is likely to be very frequent, otherwise in a year).

A sample question and method for estimating use is given below (using the Croydon test survey). The test question used to measure amount of use is:

● **How many times have you visited the library in the past year?** (CIRCLE AS APPROPRIATE.)

    1–5   6–10   11–15   16–20   more than 20

The question is visit-related, so it is not necessary to weight it by the number of users. The proportion of visits in which each of the services is used, total use and average use per user are estimated as follows:

Table 6.3

Service	Proportion of visits (%)	Total uses	Average uses per user
Stock			
Look for a specific book, magazine etc	(43.8)	82,488	1.8
Consult books/magazines for specific information	(57.6)	108,477	2.3
Read books or other library material	(15.2)	28,626	0.6
Ask librarian for help in finding information	(50.4)	94,917	2.0
Photocopy library materials	(15.5)	29,191	0.6
Use Prestel	(3.1)	5,838	0.124

At Croydon there were estimated to be 188,328 total visits in a year (see Section 6.2). The total number of uses is calculated by multiplying the estimated proportion of visits in which a service is used by the total number of visits (for example 0.438 times 188,238 = 82,488 uses of stock by looking for a specific book, magazine etc). Average number of uses per user is calculated by dividing total uses by total number of users (that is, 47,129 estimated at Croydon). If the average number of uses per user is very small, one can express the average in terms of 1,000 users. For example, there are 124 uses of Prestel per 1,000 users of the library at Croydon.

But how can we estimate the total number of uses of specific services in the manner presented above when users may use a service several times during a specific visit to the library? For example, Prestel might be used more than once during a visit. Also, for some services, the number of uses may not be as indicative of effectiveness as other measures. For example, number of materials or number of pages photocopied might be more indicative of effectiveness than number of times photocopier is used. Stock use is another example of this point. Usually public libraries have a good count of issues, but know little of how much reading is actually done in the library. An example of how to calculate this number is described below.

The number of books read during a visit is from a visit-related question not a user-related question. In this case, total visits are used for each stratum. This time, instead of each sample response being one visitor, the response may be 0 magazines read, 1 magazine read, 5 magazines read etc. The total observations for the five sample visits in the first stratum might be (0, 5, 0, 2, 3). The total number of visits in this stratum is 3,700. The total magazines read for all five visits would be 10. The total number of magazines read during all visits would be 7,500 (10 ÷ 5 × 3,500). The total number of magazines read for the remaining strata are given in Table 6.4.

Table 6.4

Strata	Sample number of visits	Total number of times magazines are read by sample	Total number of visits	Annual number of times magazines are read
Less than once a year	5	10	3,750	7,500
Once a year	10	22	7,500	16,500
Several times a year	20	48	15,000	36,000
Once a month	25	66	18,756	49,516
Twice a month	50	152	37,560	114,182
Once a month	60	201	44,928	150,509
Twice a week or more	80	295	60,000	221,250
Total	**250**	**794**	**187,494**	**595,457**

The estimated annual total number of magazine readings (that is, number of times magazines are read) in the library is 595,457. The average number of magazine readings per visit is 3.2 (595,457 ÷ 187,494 or 794 ÷ 250).

**6.4 User perception of
library service attributes,
user-expressed satisfaction
and user-indicated
importance**

It is difficult to measure user perception of library service or service output attributes, satisfaction and importance. However, one can use proxy measures through rating scales for these three measures. These rating scales can, for example, range from 1 to 4 or up to 1 to 7. There is some controversy in the survey field about whether the number of points on the scales should be an even number (for example 1, 2, 3, 4) or odd number (for example 1, 2, 3, 4, 5). It is clearly preferable to use an even number if it is desirable to force a choice from the respondent. Voter preference is an example where forcing a choice is important. The examples below use a scale of five (however, four, six or seven can be used instead).

User perception of service
attributes

It is important to measure user perception of library service performance because it has been shown that this is correlated with the extent to which services are used. It is often argued that users do not have the ability to rate performance of services. However, the perception of good or bad performance (right or wrong) still affects the extent to which the services are used. If there is evidence that users' perceptions are clearly mistaken, then the library should try to change the perceptions by public relations or some other means. Examples of rating performance are given below:

- **Please rate the quality of this library's stock of books, magazines etc.** (CIRCLE APPROPRIATE NUMBER. CIRCLE NA, IF YOU HAVE NOT USED THE STOCK.)

Very poor	Poor	Neither poor nor high	High	Very high	Not applicable
1	2	3	4	5	NA

It is generally better to specify a critical incident of service use and ask about specific attributes of service output (for example, quality, timeliness). For example one can rate the relevance of online search output:

Low relevance	Medium relevance	High relevance
1	2	3

It is also much better (but expensive and difficult to administer) to ask users of specific services to make choices between service attributes, such as relevance of online search output, response time and price (if charged). One method for determining the relative preference among service attributes is conjoint measurement. An example is given below.

Conjoint measurement provides a relative utility measure of search attributes such as quality of search, speed of response and price. Since it has been shown that the value of library services is in saving time (a scarce resource), the respondent could think of the price paid in terms of their time. The mathematical method requires respondents to rank pairwise combinations of attributes.

- In the matrix below are two attributes: quality of search (that is, high, medium and low relevance) and cost in terms of your time (that is, ½ hour, ½–1 hour, 1–2 hours). Please rank the nine combinations of levels from 1 to 9. Presumably, the highest rank (1) is high relevance at a cost of only ½ hour to you. The lowest rank (9) is low relevance at a cost to you of 1–2 hours. Please rank the remaining cells from 2 to 8.

	Cost in terms of your time		
Quality of search	½ hour	½–1 hour	1–2 hours
High relevance of items	1		
Medium relevance of items			
Low relevance of items			9

- In the matrix below, we give two other pairs of attributes: speed of response (within a day, within 3 days, over 3 days) and cost in terms of your time. Please rank the unranked cells from 2 to 8.

	Cost in terms of your time		
Speed of response	½ hour	½–1 hour	1–2 hours
Within a day	1		
Within 3 days			
Over 3 days			9

- In the matrix below, we give the last combination of pairs of attributes: quality of search and speed of response. Please rank the unranked cells from 2 to 8.

	Quality of search		
Speed of response	High relevance	Medium relevance	Low relevance
Within a day	1		
Within 3 days			
Over 3 days			9

The conjoint measurement method requires users of services such as online searching to make judgements about sets of alternatives involving different combinations of search output attributes: quality, timeliness and price. The output attribute of quality of search can be specified at three levels: high, medium and low relevance of items retrieved. Timeliness can also be specified to three levels: speed of response within a day, between one and three days and over three days. Cost in terms of user time can be measured at three levels: ½ hour, ½–1 hour, and 1–2 hours. These times can then be converted into monetary units for analysis and display, resulting in the levels £25, £75 and £125 respectively.

Figure 6.2

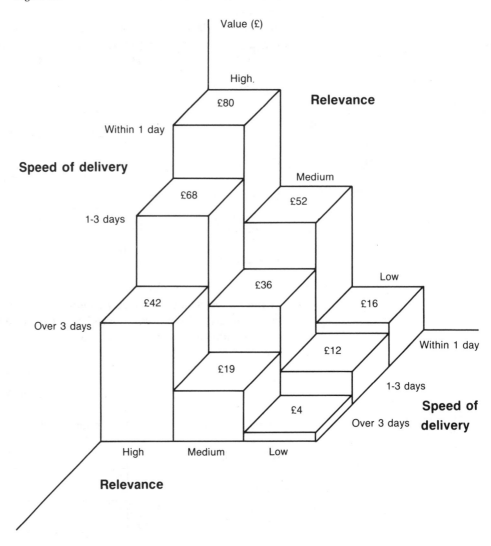

The relative value of quality and timeliness is expressed in Figure 6.2. This figure shows the monetary value of all nine combinations of levels of relevance and speed of delivery. If search results are returned within one day, but relevance of items retrieved drops from high to medium, the value decreases from £80 to £52. Similarly, if relevance remains high but response time drops from within one day to between one and three days, the value drops from £80 to £68. Thus, over all combinations of these two performance attributes, it is estimated that the value of quality is greater to the user than the speed of delivery, although both are appreciable. We can see that low relevance of items retrieved, and response times of over three days, reduce value to only an estimated £4. Clearly, both quality and timeliness of response should be kept at a high level when at all possible.

User-expressed satisfaction

Satisfaction is a good indicator of the perception of service performance, and level of satisfaction is generally correlated with frequency of visits to public libraries. For example, the test survey of Croydon yielded the results shown in Table 6.5.

Library users tend to respond favourably to public library services. However, both the proportions of users who indicate they are very dissatisfied and dissatisfied, and the average ratings, are good indicators of service performance. Furthermore, if you give users the opportunity to say why they are dissatisfied with the service, it will help you to address problems.

An example is given below for calculating user-expressed satisfaction. First the estimates of proportion of users satisfied and average ratings of satisfaction are calculated using weights for number of visits strata. For example, 63 of 134 respondents (from the Croydon test survey who answered the stock satisfaction

Table 6.5 Average number of visits

	Dissatisfied or very dissatisfied	Neither satisfied nor dissatisfied	Satisfied or very satisfied
Collection of books and other materials	2.7	3.2	4.3
Approachability and responsiveness of staff	2.2	2.7	4.2
Ability of staff to help locate information and materials	2.2	2.5	4.3

question) indicated they visited the library one to five times in the past year. These 63 visitors rated their satisfaction with the stock as shown in Table 6.6.

Table 6.6 Satisfaction with stock of visitors who visited library 1–5 times in the past year

	Sample	Proportion (%)	Total
Very dissatisfied	3	(4.8)	1,892
Dissatisfied	1	(1.6)	631
Neither satisfied nor dissatisfied	11	(17.5)	6,899
Satisfied	35	(55.5)	21,880
Very satisfied	13	(20.6)	8,121
Total	**63**	**(100.0)**	**39,423**

The proportion of users who rated satisfaction at the five levels was calculated directly (for example 3 ÷ 63 = 0.048 or 4.8%). The total was then calculated by multiplying the proportion (for example, 0.048) by the stratum total (for example, 39,423), yielding the estimated total (for example 1,892). Table 6.7 gives the totals for all strata.

Table 6.7

Strata	Very dissatisfied	Dissatisfied	Neither satisfied nor dissatisfied	Satisfied	Very satisfied	Total
1–5	1,892	631	6,899	21,880	8,121	39,423
6–10	0	0	357	3,220	1,250	4,827
11–15	0	0	0	884	665	1,549
16–20	0	79	0	475	0	554
>20	0	0	135	303	338	776
Total	**1,892**	**710**	**7,391**	**26,762**	**10,374**	**47,129**
Proportion (%)	**(0.040)**	**(0.015)**	**(0.157)**	**(0.568)**	**(0.220)**	**(1.000)**

So, 22.0% of the users are estimated to be very satisfied and 78.8% satisfied or very satisfied with the stock and 5.5% dissatisfied or very dissatisfied.

Average satisfaction is calculated by cross-multiplying (a) the proportions above and (b) values given for satisfaction ratings: very dissatisfied (1), dissatisfied (2), neither satisfied nor dissatisfied (3), satisfied (4) and very satisfied (5). Average rating is 3.91 (that is, $0.040 \times 1 + 0.015 \times 2 + 0.157 \times 3 + 0.568 \times 4 + 0.220 \times 5$). Thus, the average rating (3.91) is just below satisfied (4). Typically, satisfaction with stock is lower than with other services. Also, satisfaction ratings for services in general tend to be higher than satisfaction asked for critical incidents of service use (for example how satisfied are you with your last search?) and with attributes of service output (for example how satisfied are you with speed of response to your last request for a search?).

User-indicated importance

There are advantages to knowing how important users consider a service, as well as their view of that service's performance or how satisfied they are with it. For example, we will not be so concerned by low satisfaction ratings where users think that a service is not very important. We can measure satisfaction, either with the service as a whole, or with its output attributes, using rating scales:

Very unimportant	Unimportant	Neither important nor unimportant	Important	Very important
1	2	3	4	5

Calculations can be done as shown above for satisfaction ratings. Services can be compared with one another for satisfaction and importance separately, by multiplying averages (ranging from 1 – very unimportant and very dissatisfied, to 5 – very important and very satisfied), or by multiplying each response (1 to 5) and averaging the resulting products across responses.

6.5 Value of public library services

There are several measures or indicators of the value of public library services including the number of visits to the public library, number of uses of library services, purposes for which public libraries are used and user time spent getting to the library and using its services.

Number of visits and uses were discussed earlier. One can argue that the more a public library is used the greater its value. Thus, cost per visit and cost per use of specific library services are good indicators of return on investment in public libraries and their services. These indicators are best calculated by dividing total cost by total visits (or uses, if appropriate).

Purpose of use

The purposes for which public libraries are used include:

- meeting personal needs in solving day-to-day problems, assisting in coping with trauma or crises, being informed of news and current events, and so on;

- accommodating needs in entertainment, hobbies, recreation and leisure-time activities;

- enhancing lifelong learning;

- supporting work or career.

These uses affect the local economy and/or the quality of life of users.

The Tameside survey test provides data for an example of how to calculate the proportion of users who use the public library for various purposes. In this example there is no existing or survey data for total visits to the library or total users of the library. The number of visits per year are determined from the following visitor survey responses:

- **How often do you usually visit the public library?** (CIRCLE ONE.)

		Weight
This is my first visit	1	Average
Less than once a year	2	0.02
Once a year	3	0.04
Several times a year	4	0.25
Once a month	5	0.50
Twice a month	6	1.00
Once a week	7	2.00
Twice a week or more	8	4.00

The data were collected over a two-week period so approximate weighting is as shown above. The weights reflect the number of times a user would be expected to be in the library in the two-week study period. Those who visit once a week would be expected to be in the library twice during the survey period so they are given a weight of 2.00. Those who come once a month would have one out of two chances to be in the library during that two-week period, thus they are given a weight of 0.50. If it is a user's first visit we can use the average number of visits across all visitors.

In effect, each sample observation is divided by the weight in the appropriate stratum (that is, 0.50 for the once a month stratum). For example, to estimate the proportion of users who visit once a year etc, we divide each of the number of responses in each of the strata by the weights (for example $5 \div 0.02 = 250$) and divide the adjusted responses by the new total of all adjusted responses (for example $250 \div 1,972 = 0.127$ or 12.7% – see Table 6.8).

The proportion of users who visit the library once a year is estimated to be 7.6%, twice a week or more is 3.1%, and so on.

Table 6.8

	Number of responses	Weight	Adjusted responses	Proportion (%)
Less than once a year	5	0.02*	250	(12.7)
Once a year	6	0.04	150	(7.6)
Several times a year	121	0.25	484	(24.5)
Once a month	249	0.50	498	(25.3)
Twice a month	352	1.00	352	(17.8)
Once a week	352	2.00	176	(8.9)
Twice a week or more	249	4.00	62	(3.1)
Total	**1,351**		**1,972**	**(100.0)**

* The amount judged to be one half of once a year.

The proportion of users who use the library for the purposes mentioned earlier is determined from the following question:

- **What are the two most important purposes for which you use the public library?**
  (CIRCLE MOST IMPORTANT AND SECOND MOST IMPORTANT.)

	Most important	Second most important
For information or materials related to school and college	1	2
For information or materials related to job or career	1	2
For information related to personal interests or needs	1	2
To borrow reading materials for leisure time use	1	2
To acquire other materials (records, cassettes etc) for leisure time use	1	2
Something else (please specify)	1	2

Results, using weighted estimates because the question is user-related, are given in Table 6.9.

Table 6.9

Purpose of use	Most important (%)	Second most important (%)
For information or materials related to school or college	6.7	5.7
For information or materials related to job or career	4.4	8.4
For information related to personal interests or needs	25.0	48.4
To borrow reading materials for leisure time use	59.7	25.9
To acquire other materials (records, cassettes etc) for leisure time use	4.0	11.1
Something else	0.2	0.7
Total	**100.0**	**100.2**

Table 6.9 shows that for this particular library user community, the leisure time purpose of use is prevalent but all purposes of use are valuable to some degree.

Time is a measure of value

One means of characterising the value of public library services is the time users are willing to spend going to and using the library. If people spend time in library-related activities, this shows that they value information provided by the public library. The greater the time 'price' they are willing to pay, the greater the value.

In fact access (that is, distance) is related to users' time. Often, as the time (distance) is increased the use of the library decreases because the 'price' increases. In much the same manner demand for consumer products decreases with increased price. (However, use does not clearly decrease with time/distance for either of the two survey test sites: Tameside and Croydon.) Methods for calculating estimates of the time taken to get to the library and time spent in the library are discussed below.

Travel time

At Tameside the average amount of time taken to get to the library is based on the following question:

- **How long did it take you to get to the library?**
  -------- minutes

This question is visit-related (not user-related) and therefore it is not necessary to stratify by number of visits. The tallies for responses are given in Table 6.10.

Table 6.10

Response (minutes)	Number of responses	Response (minutes)	Number of responses
1	14	15	190
2	62	17	2
3	56	18	5
4	29	20	114
5	315	25	16
6	9	30	56
7	17	35	5
8	14	40	7
9	1	45	2
10	310	50	1
11	2	60	4
12	5	90	1
13	4	220	1

In this example:

Total sample size = total number of responses = 1,242

Total responses = 14,004 minutes (that is, $1 \times 14 + 2 \times 63 + 3 \times 56$ etc = 14,004)

$$\text{Average distance in time} = \frac{\text{Total responses}}{\text{Total sample size}}$$

$$= \frac{14,004}{1,242} = 11.3 \text{ minutes per visit}$$

Median time = 10.3 minutes per visit (that is, there are as many visits below that time as took longer than it. The median value is the middle value.)

The precision of the estimated average is given by the standard error which is easily calculated by the following equation:

$$\text{Standard error} = \sqrt{\frac{\Sigma (x - \bar{x})^2}{n (n-1)}}$$

To calculate this on a hand calculator:

Subtract the average (11.3) from the response (for example $1 - 11.3 = -10.3$).

Square the number (for example $-10.3 \times -10.3 = 106.09$).

Multiply the result by number of responses (for example $14 \times 106.09 = 1,485.26$).

Add to the memory.

Do this for all responses from 1 to 220.

Divide the total in the memory (the numerator (123,071.92) by the sample size n ($123,071.92$) ÷ by $1,242 = 99.09$).

Divide the result by n−1 (99.09 ÷ by $1,241 = 0.080$).

Take the square root of this number to obtain the standard error (0.28).

Thus, the confidence interval of the estimated average 11.3 is ± 0.28 at 0.68 level of confidence, or 11.3 ± 0.55 at 0.95 level of confidence (see Appendix A.3.1.3 for more details of the meaning of confidence intervals and how to calculate them).

Note that most of the visits are made from home (89.5%), with remaining visits made from work (5.3%) or shops (3.4%). The average distance travelled is 1.2 miles, with the principal mode of travel being on foot (56%), then car (34%) and bus (9%).

Time spent in the library

Time spent in the library is observed using the following questions:

- **At approximately what time did you arrive at the library today?**
  -------- am
    or
  -------- pm

- **At approximately what time will you leave the library today?**
  -------- am
    or
  -------- pm

Estimate by calculating the time gap between when a user arrives and leaves. It is invalid to make this estimate by subtracting average arrival time from average departure time. The average for this estimate is made from visit-related, not user-related, responses, and thus estimates are not weighted by number of users in number of visits strata.

At Tameside, 1,162 visitors responded to this question. The average length of visit is 35.5 minutes (with the average amount of time ranging from 30 minutes to 44 minutes among branch libraries). Thus, the overall average time spent by users is 58.1 minutes per visit, that is, 11.3 minutes travelling to the library, 11.3 minutes returning and 35.5 minutes in the library. When we consider the average number of visits, the annual average amount of time spent in the library works out at nearly 16 hours per year per user. Note that this ignores the amount of time spent reading the materials, which in a sense is the value of the information found in the documents.

6.6 Hand tabulations	Sometimes it may be necessary for a public library to hand tabulate in order to estimate totals, averages or proportions. Two examples of hand tabulations are presented below: one for estimating averages, means and totals, and the other for estimating proportions and totals. Data obtained from the Croydon test survey are used in the examples. In both instances the estimates are made from stratified samples. (See Appendix A for a discussion on stratified samples.) Thus, the tabulation form must reflect the strata.

Example 1: Estimating averages, means and totals

The first example involves estimates of the amount of time required for visitors to get to the public library. The data were collected using a visitor survey. The question was asked in the following way:

- **How long did it take you to get to the Information Centre?**
  -------- minutes

Visitors were sampled over different time periods during the weekdays and on Saturday. Because the proportion of sampling in the time period varied and since distance or time travelled may vary by the time of day, the data are tabulated by the four time of day strata, that is, 9.30–13.00, 13.00–16.00, 16.00–close, Saturday. Table 6.11 is an example of a tabulation form. (Note that actual data from only one stratum is displayed.)

An estimated average from a stratified sample is calculated by estimating the total minutes for each stratum, summing total minutes from the four strata, and dividing by the total number of visits. Steps in this calculation are as follows:

> Add all of the observations in each stratum (for example 1,347 minutes in the 9.30–13.00 stratum).
>
> Count the sample in each stratum (for example 80 visitors in the 9.30–13.00 stratum).
>
> Determine the population of visits in each stratum (for example there were 610 visits over the one-week sampling period between 9.30–13.00; total population of visits is 610 × 52 = 31,720 visits).
>
> Estimate total of visits minutes in each stratum by multiplying the population total by sample total divided by sample size (for example, 31,720 × 1,347 ÷ 80 = 534,086 in the 9.30–13.00 stratum).
>
> Add the four strata population of visits (for example 188,344 visits).
>
> Add the four strata total minutes (for example 3,226,269 minutes).
>
> Divide strata total by population of visits (for example, 3,226,269 ÷ 188,344 = 17.1 minutes per visit).

The estimated average time taken to get to the public library is 17.1 minutes.

As it turns out it was probably not necessary to stratify by time of day because the differences in average time among the strata were not appreciable. In fact, the unweighted average is 16.7 minutes, not much less than the weighted average 17.1 minutes.

The statistical precision of the estimated average is calculated using the equation below:

$$\text{Standard error} = \sqrt{\frac{\Sigma \, (x - \bar{x})^2}{n \, (n-1)}}$$

Estimating the median

The responses above for time required to get to the library are arrayed in Table 6.12.

The median is 15.2 minutes. That is, one-half of the visits take less than 15.2 minutes and one-half take more than that amount of time. The least amount of time is one minute and the greatest amount is 10 hours (600 minutes).

Table 6.11

Tabulation made: Question 16: How long did it take you to get to the Information Centre?
Date: 01/18/89   Tabulator: DWK

	9.30-13.00	13.00-16.00	16.00-Close	Saturday	Total
	10, 2, 27, 10 10, 45, 4, 5 25, 14, 20, 30 5, 15, 10, 30 1, 10, 20, 5 10, 10, 3, 30 20, 15, 20, 25 40, 20, 2, 30 8, 30, 5, 10 20, 30, 5, 2 45, 10, 30, 25 15, 20, 30, 15 5, 10, 20, 30 1, 10, 45, 20 10, 15, 40, 20 8, 5, 10, 5 40, 30, 15, 5 5, 15, 30, 5 10, 45, 30, 5 1, 30, 2, 2				
Sample total	1,347	832	228	110	2,517 min
Sample size	80	53	13	5	151 visits
Population	31,720	65,936	75,764	14,924	188,344 visits
Total	534,086	1,035,071	1,328,784	328,328	3,226,269 min
Average	16,8	15,7	17.5	22.0	17.1 min

Outliers

It may be best to discount the 10-hour trip to the library because the respondent may have visited town for other purposes and then gone to the library. The amount of time is certainly not typical and affects the average distance by nearly four minutes. The value is considered an outlier and, therefore, can be dropped from the calculations, as was done in the example above.

Table 6.12

Sample response (minutes)	Number of responses
1	8
2	9
3	5
4	3
5	19
8	2
10	26
14	1
15	17
17	1
20	22
25	5
27	1
30	19
40	4
45	7
50	1
120	1
600	1
Total	**152**

If one observation stands out as an outlier and is over three standard deviations greater than the average, it is considered statistically valid to disregard that observation in calculations. The estimated standard deviation is 14.8 minutes (see below for how to calculate the standard deviation). There standard deviations total 44.4 minutes. Since the average is 16.7 minutes, 600 minutes is far more than three standard deviations above the average.

Standard error

The standard error can be simply calculated from the array above. In the standard error equation the difficult part of the calculation is:

$$\Sigma \, (x - \bar{x})^2$$

where x is the sample response. For the example, x would be 1, 2, 3, minutes etc. The average is x, which is 16.7 minutes for the unweighted data above. Standard error can be calculated as follows (excluding the outlier of 600 minutes) – see Table 6.13.

The right-hand column is calculated by multiplying $(x - \bar{x})^2$ by the number of responses (for example 8) since that calculation would normally be done eight times based on the equation above. The next steps are to:

Divide the total $\Sigma \, (x - \bar{x})^2$ by the sample size (for example 32,923.99 ÷ 151 = 218.04).

Divide the resulting number by $n - 1$ (for example 218.04 ÷ 150 = 1.45).

Take the square root of that number (for example $\sqrt{1.45} = 1.2$).

So, the standard error of the average time spent getting to the library is 1.2 minutes. The confidence interval is:

16.7 ± 1.2 minutes at 0.68 level of confidence

16.7 ± 2.4 minutes at 0.95 level of confidence

(See Appendix A for a detailed explanation of standard error, confidence intervals and level of confidence.)

Table 6.13

Sample response (x minutes)	$(x - \bar{x})$	$(x - \bar{x})^2$	Number of responses	$\Sigma\,(x - \bar{x})^2$
1	−15.7	246.49	8	1,971.92
2	−14.7	216.09	9	1,944.81
3	−13.7	187.69	5	938.45
4	−12.7	161.29	3	483.87
5	−11.7	136.89	19	2,600.91
8	−8.7	75.69	2	151.38
10	−6.7	44.89	26	1,167.14
14	−2.7	7.29	1	7.29
15	−1.7	2.89	17	49.13
17	−0.7	0.49	1	0.49
20	3.3	10.89	22	239.58
25	8.3	68.89	5	344.45
27	10.3	106.09	1	106.09
30	13.3	176.89	19	3,360.91
40	23.3	542.89	4	2,171.56
45	28.3	800.89	7	5,606.23
50	33.3	1,108.89	1	1,108.89
120	103.3	10,670.89	1	10,670.89
Total	—	—	**151**	**32,923.99**

Standard deviation

The standard deviation is calculated by taking the square root of the number found in the first step above:

for example $\sqrt{218.04} = 14.8$.

Example 2: Estimating proportions

The second example of hand tabulation also uses data from the Croydon test survey. Here estimates are of the proportions of users who rate their satisfaction with the library's collection at five levels. The question can be asked as follows:

● **How satisfied are you with the Information Centre's stock of books and other materials?** (CIRCLE AS APPROPRIATE.)

Very dissatisfied	Dissatisfied	Neither satisfied nor dissatisfied	Satisfied	Very satisfied
1	2	3	4	5

Hand tabulate the results as shown in Table 6.14.

Stratify the survey results into classes of number of visits to estimate the number of users (see Section 6.2 for an explanation of why and how this is done).

For each stratum, calculate a weight by dividing the population of users in each stratum by the sample size in each stratum. The weights are calculated for the example in Table 6.15.

Record the weights on the tabulation form for reference.

On the tabulation form is space for recording the number of respondents reporting various levels of satisfaction. Recording is most easily done by first separating the questionnaires into stacks of the five strata. Calculate proportions by the following steps:

Count the number of responses in each stratum and level of satisfaction cell (for example 3 in very dissatisfied/1–5 visits) and multiply that number by the appropriate weight (for example $3 \times 625.8 = 1,877.4$).

Record this number in the appropriate population space.

Add all the populations in the columns (for example 1,877.4 in the first column, $625.8 + 79.1 = 704.9$ etc).

Table 6.14

Tabulation made: How satisfied are you with the Information Centre's stock of books and other materials?
Date: 01/18/89   Tabulator: DWK

Strata (visits)	Very dis-satisfied	Dis satisfied	Neither satisfied nor dis-satisfied	Satisfied	Very satisfied	Total
1-5 Wt = Population	3 1,874.4	1 625.8	11 6,883.8	35 21,903.0	13 8,135.4	63
6-10 Wt = Population	0	0	2 357.6	18 3,218.4	7 1,251.6	27
11-15 Wt = Population	0	0	8	8 884.8	6 663.6	14
16-20 Wt = Population	0	1 79.1	0	6 474.6	0	7
Over 20 Wt = Population	0	0	4 134,8	9 303,3	10 337.0	23
Total	1,877.4	704.9	7,376,2	26,784,1	10,387,6	47,130
Proportion	4.0	1.5	15.7	56.8	22.0	100.0%

Cross-Multiply   0.040   0.030   0.471   2.272   1.100   3.913

Sum the totals for the five levels of satisfaction to get the total number of users (for example, 1,877.4 + 704.9 etc = 47,130).

Divide each total by the total number of users and convert to percentages (for example 1,877.4 ÷ 47,130 = 0.0398 × 100 = 3.98%).

Thus about 22% of the users are very satisfied with the stock, 3.98% are very dissatisfied, and so on. By treating the ratings of satisfactions as scores (that is, very dissatisfied – 1, dissatisfied – 2 etc) we can calculate average satisfaction ratings by cross-multiplying the scores (at the top of the table) by the appropriate proportions

Table 6.15

Strata (visits)	Population of users	Sample	Weight
1–5	39,423	63	625.8
6–10	4,827	27	178.8
11–15	1,549	14	110.6
16–20	554	7	79.1
Over 20	776	23	33.7
Total	**47,129**	**134**	

(at the bottom part of the table) and adding them across levels of satisfaction as follows:

Multiply the scores by the proportions (for example, $1 \times 0.040 = 0.040$).

Add the results across the five levels of satisfaction columns (for example $0.040 + 0.030$ etc $= 3.913$).

Thus, the average satisfaction rating for the stock is 3.91.

Standard errors can be computed for both the proportion of users who are very dissatisfied etc, and for average ratings. A simplified equation (ignoring stratification) for the proportions is:

$$\text{Standard error} = \sqrt{\frac{pq}{n}}$$

where: p is the proportion of interest
q is $1-p$
n is the sample size

Thus, the standard error for the proportion of users very dissatisfied is:

$$\text{Standard error} = \sqrt{\frac{(0.04)\,(0.96)}{134}}$$

$$= 0.017$$

The confidence interval is:

0.040 ± 0.017 at 0.68 level of confidence
OR
0.040 ± 0.033 at 0.95 level of confidence

Table 6.16 shows other standard errors.

Table 6.16

	Proportion (%)	Standard error
Very dissatisfied	(0.040)	0.017
Dissatisfied	(0.015)	0.011
Neither satisfied nor dissatisfied	(0.157)	0.031
Satisfied	(0.568)	0.043
Very satisfied	(0.220)	0.036

The standard error for average satisfaction rating is:

$$\text{Standard error} = \sqrt{\frac{\Sigma \, (x - \bar{x})^2}{n \, (n-1)}}$$

Calculations are in Table 6.17.

Table 6.17

Sample response (Satisfaction ratings)	$(x - \bar{x})$	$(x - \bar{x})^2$	Number of responses	$\Sigma \, (x - \bar{x})^2$
1	−2.91	8.47	3	25.41
2	−1.91	3.65	2	7.30
3	−0.91	0.83	17	14.11
4	0.09	0.01	76	0.76
5	1.09	1.19	36	42.77
Total	—	—	**134**	**90.35**

To calculate the standard error of the average satisfaction ratings:

Divide the total $(x - \bar{x})^2$ by the sample size (for example 90.35 ÷ 134 = 0.674).

Divide the resulting number by $n - 1$ (for example 0.674 ÷ 133 = 0.00507).

Take the square root of that number ($\sqrt{0.00507} = 0.071$).

The standard error in the example is 0.055 and the confidence interval is:

3.91 ± 0.071 at 0.68 level of confidence
    OR
3.91 ± 0.139 at 0.95 level of confidence.

6.7 Calculating derived indicators

Another type of calculation is needed to relate averages of one measure to varying levels of another measure. Examples include:

- Cost by attribute levels
- Productivity by attribute levels
- Amount of use by attribute levels
- Satisfaction by attribute levels
- Amount of use by satisfaction levels
- Cost by satisfaction levels.

An example of how to calculate such indicators is given below.

In most instances one of the two measures used in the calculation of performance indicators is dependent on the other measure. For example, with *Cost per output* the amount of cost is directly dependent on the amount of output; with *Amount of use by attribute levels* the amount of use is directly dependent on quality, timeliness etc of services. All of the performance indicators are derived with these dependencies in mind.

There are basically three ways in which performance indicators are calculated:

- dividing one measure by another (averages or totals)
- displaying the derived indicators across levels or amounts of one of the two measures
- displaying averages of measures across levels of another measure.

These three general methods are discussed below with some examples given.

Dividing one measure by another

Indicators which can be calculated by dividing one measure by another are:

- *Productivity* (output quantities divided by input costs)
- *Cost per output* (inverse of productivity)
- *Turnover rate* (amount of use divided by output quantities)
- *User satisfaction* (total ratings divided by number of ratings)
- *Cost per use* (input costs divided by amount of use)
- *Cost per user* (input costs divided by number of users)
- *Cost per capita* (input costs divided by number of persons in service population)
- *Users as a proportion of population* (number of users divided by number of persons in service population)
- *Use per capita* (amount of use divided by number of persons in service population)
- *Needs fill rate* (number of needs filled divided by number of needs identified).

Note that the values calculated can be either totals or averages (since the average in the numerator is based on the same number as the average in the denominator).

Displaying indicators across levels or amounts of one of the two measures from which they are derived

It is useful to display derived indicators across levels or amounts of one of the two measures (for example to establish economies of scale). Two examples of such displays are:

- *Cost per output* displayed across levels of output
- *Cost per user* displayed across levels of user group size.

Data observed in a recent study show that such relationships exist and it is useful to know them.

An example of economies of scale involves interlibrary loan request processing to determine its disposition. Examining the *Cost per output* of 76 library systems reveals the information in Table 6.18.

Table 6.18

Number of requests processed	Cost per output (£)
Under 1,000	3.52
1,000–2,500	1.89
2,500–5,000	0.91
5,000–15,000	0.49
15,000–20,000	0.71
Over 20,000	0.71

If, for example, a public library has branches that require under about 5,000 to 10,000 interlibrary loan requests to be processed, it would appear that these requests could be processed less expensively in a central operation.

In another example, it has been observed that *Cost per user* of certain technical processing functions decreases as the size of the population served increases. This is shown in Table 6.19.

Table 6.19

Size of population served	Cost per user (£)
Less than 800	7.30
800–1,500	4.72
1,501–2,500	1.98
2,501–4,500	1.66
4,501–7,500	1.93
7,501–15,000	0.88
Over 15,000	1.48

Although it is difficult to know *why* such a relationship exists, it is important to know whether or not it *does* exist.

Displaying averages of measures across levels of another measure

To calculate some performance indicators which involve such measures, it is necessary to make observations in the library and to ask users about critical incidents of use. For example, one performance indicator is the average cost per level of satisfaction with a service output such as relevance of online search output.

To calculate such a performance indicator, choose a sample of online searches and obtain measures of cost and user satisfaction for each search. An example of 30 such observations might be as shown in Table 6.20.

Table 6.20

Sample	Search cost in time (hours)	User satisfaction rating	Sample	Search cost in time (hours)	User satisfaction rating
1	1.2	5	16	0.4	2
2	0.6	4	17	1.1	5
3	0.7	2	18	0.7	1
4	0.9	5	19	0.6	4
5	1.0	4	20	0.4	3
6	0.5	3	21	1.6	5
7	0.8	2	22	0.3	1
8	0.2	1	23	0.6	3
9	0.8	5	24	0.8	3
10	0.8	4	25	0.9	5
11	0.4	2	26	0.9	4
12	0.3	2	27	1.4	5
13	0.9	3	28	0.7	3
14	0.9	5	29	0.5	2
15	0.6	1	30	0.8	4

Table 6.21 shows the costs arranged by satisfaction levels.

Table 6.21

Satisfaction level	Sample observations	Average cost/search
Very dissatisfied – 1	0.2, 0.6, 0.7, 0.3	0.45 hrs/search
Dissatisfied – 2	0.7, 0.8, 0.4, 0.3, 0.4, 0.5	0.52 hrs/search
Neither dissatisfied nor satisfied – 3	0.5, 0.9, 0.4, 0.6, 0.8, 0.7	0.65 hrs/search
Satisfied – 4	0.6, 1.0, 0.8, 0.6, 0.9, 0.8	0.78 hrs/search
Very satisfied – 5	1.2, 0.9, 0.8, 0.9, 1.1, 1.6, 0.9, 1.4	1.10 hrs/search

Such evidence (if available) would suggest that substantial cost in terms of searcher time is required to achieve high levels of satisfaction, particularly to achieve ratings of 'Very satisfied'. This is important because user satisfaction ratings have been demonstrated to be related to amount of use, which is an indicator of the value of a public library.

Appendix A. Understanding the methods

A.1 Introduction

Sections 5 and 6 of the manual described and demonstrated methods of collecting data and calculating measures and indicators. This appendix aims to help you understand any principles underlying the methods with which you may not be familiar. The emphasis is on cost concepts (for example, fixed and variable costs, allocation and depreciation) and statistical and survey methods.

A.2 How to obtain input and output measures

This subsection discusses methods that might be used for obtaining input and output measures. As we have stressed frequently throughout this manual, it is essential that input and output measures are obtained within a common context. One aspect of this is that you should measure common services and operational functions for both input and output.

A.2.1 Examples of services and operational functions

Below are examples of services and functions that are often performed in public libraries. These examples are given for 19 principal services and functions and a total of 46 basic activities.

Services/functions

- Stock development and management
  1. Stock development
  2. Stock weeding

- Acquisitions
  3. Ordering
  4. Processing stock received
  5. Chasing
  6. Cancellations

- Post processing
  7. Post processing

- Cataloguing
  8. Copy and enhanced cataloguing
  9. Original cataloguing

- Catalogue maintenance
  10. Catalogue additions activities
  11. Catalogue withdrawal activities

- Physical processing
  12. Spine labelling, barcode labelling/linking
  13. Other physical processing
  14. Monograph binding and repair
  15. Acquisitions list

- Periodicals binding
  16. Prepare binding records
  17. Preparing materials to be bound
  18. Processing returned bound volumes

- Invoice processing
  19. Invoice processing

- Reference services
  20. Directional
  21. Reference

- Online bibliographic searching
  22. Quick look-up
  23. In-depth

- Issues
  24. Issues

- Shelving and reshelving
  25. Shelving and reshelving

- Interlibrary borrowing and lending
  26. Interlibrary borrowing
  27. Interlibrary lending

- Outreach services
  28. Making contacts
  29. Performing services

- Activities
  30. Preparing for activities
  31. Conducting activities

- Photocopy services
  32. Making photocopies
  33. Providing photocopy machines
  34. Providing maintenance and supply

- Equipment services
  35. Providing instruction
  36. Maintenance and upkeep

- Public relations
  37. Preparing exhibits and promotional materials
  38. Conduct tours and/or present briefings

- Management and administration
  39. General administration
  40. Secretarial/clerical related activities
  41. Planning
  42. Statistical and financial management
  43. Personnel management and staff development
  44. Computer, equipment and systems related activities
  45. Facilities management
  46. Contract services.

At least 500 detailed activities have been identified in typical libraries. It is neither practical nor necessary to record the amount of labour time or other input costs devoted to this many activities. On the other hand, it is useful to record the time required to perform the three to ten or so basic activities performed by each employee. The basic activities must include any of the 46 mentioned above, when done by an employee. However, other important activities should be included as well; particularly if they are of interest to the employee's supervisor.

A.2.2 Cost concepts

Service input costs are defined as the cost of resources applied to public library services.

A.2.2.1 Introducing important cost concepts	Examples of resources include:

- financial resources
- staff
- facilities
- equipment and systems
- all other resources (for example, furniture, supplies).

Each service requires one or more of the resources above. For example, online database searching requires reference and support staff, space for staff and service, terminals and peripheral equipment, reference and searching materials, and so on. Generally, these resources are quantified as:

- financial amounts budgeted for services
- number of staff or staff hours applied to services
- amount of space allocated to services
- number of equipment items and systems used to provide services
- number of stock items applied or used.

Sometimes we only need to know the staff or equipment time used for a service. Often we need to know the total resources applied to a service. Then, the amount of all resources applied to services can be converted into a common unit – which is money or funds. Once we know the amount of resources applied to services, we can convert to money value through the following types of measures:

- wages, salaries or other compensation applied to services;
- amount of space rent or depreciated expenditures applied to premises;
- equipment and system lease or depreciated expenditures;
- price and cost of processing of stock items applied or used.

It is useful to identify attributes of resources and to carry them through measures of service input and output because decisions may be required concerning the attributes. Attributes of a resource or service are inherent characteristics (for example, education level of staff) or of a service (for example subject of reference searches). For example, we may wish to establish productivity (for example output quantities divided by input costs) for grades of staff such as professional librarians or support staff.

The resources applied need to be considered in a broader context:

- services, functions or activities for which the resources are used (for example for total operation of the library, lending stock, reference);
- a time period (commonly a year, although other periods, for example a month, may be appropriate for specific problems and decisions).

The context depends on the purpose for which the input measures will be used. The important thing is that *the context should be exactly the same for both input costs and output quantities and attributes*. We must be clear about what we are measuring and why we are measuring it, otherwise performance and other indicators cannot be properly interpreted.

A.2.2.2 Direct and indirect costs	Do not try to be precise (reasonably accurate but not precise). Often we must measure the cost of resources for a service by working out how resources were allocated between several services or functions. For example, a staff member may spend time on reference, interlibrary lending and administration. Thus, this person (or someone else) must estimate the amount of time spent on each service. Unless the person is observed constantly, it is necessary to rely on memory and interpretation.

Fortunately, most purposes for which input costs are measured simply do not require precise measurement and the methods of measuring proposed here and elsewhere are sufficient. The same applies to the application of equipment, facilities and most other resources. Determining the application of all funds in a public library over an annual budget period may require annual audits. When audits are required obviously exact measures are essential.

Direct costs are the resources applied which are easily identified with a service (for example line charges for an online search). Thus, direct cost is a cost which is readily associated with a service (for example interlibrary lending) or resource (for example staff).

Indirect costs are those which are not easily assignable or readily attributable to any one service or function, activity, or resource. Rosenberg (and others) subdivides indirect costs into two categories:

- *Indirect operating costs* — These costs include centrally budgeted items (for example utilities, rent, insurance) that are necessary to the general operation and maintenance of the library system.[1]

- *Indirect support costs* — Costs for support services that benefit overall administration of the library system and its services (for example administration, accounting, personnel).[1]

The key to separating direct from indirect costs is to see whether changes in amount of services appreciably affect such costs. *Direct costs vary with changes in amounts of service, while indirect costs do not.* The indirect costs can be allocated equitably in proportion to amount of direct costs (see section on measuring input costs in A.2.2.1).

A.2.2.3 Fixed and variable costs

Cost finding also involves fixed costs, semi-fixed costs, variable costs, and incremental costs. Total cost of a service normally consists of the sum cost of a number of resources such as fines, staff, equipment, facilities. Sometimes the resources are applied to the service when the service is requested or used. That is, these costs vary when the service is used and are, therefore, called variable costs. In other instances, resources are purchased or leased for applying to services over a period of time. However, once the expense is incurred, it does not matter how many times the resource is used, the cost is fixed and does not vary.

Furthermore, use essentially does not deplete the resource (except when used extensively). An example of use depleting a resource is paper used for photocopies. The cost of paper is a variable cost. Yet the use of the photocopier does not deplete the photocopier as a resource (although use can be denied for a period of time). This is a fixed cost.

There are two kinds of fixed costs: one-time fixed costs and recurring fixed costs:

- *One-time fixed costs* represent resources that are purchased outright such as stock and equipment.

- *Recurring fixed costs* represent costs that are fixed for short time periods (for example a month) but recur over the time periods. Examples of recurring fixed costs are monthly payments of equipment leases and facility rent,[2] annual fees paid to vendors or annual subscription prices paid to publishers.

Total cost of public library services is the sum of fixed and variable costs incurred for the services. Obviously total cost increases as the amount of service transactions (or units provided) increases. Figure A.1 provides an example of how total cost of a service increases with number of transactions for that service.

- If there are no transactions the total cost would be the sum of fixed costs applied to the service such as terminals, facilities, or stock.

- If there are transactions there would be an incremental cost for the resources

---

[1] Definition of some terms adopted from *Cost Finding for Public Libraries*, Philip Rosenberg, American Library Association, 1985.

[2] One could also think of staff salaries as recurring fixed costs, but there are reasons for not doing so, one of which is that personnel can be redeployed if they cannot be usefully applied to a service.

Figure A.1

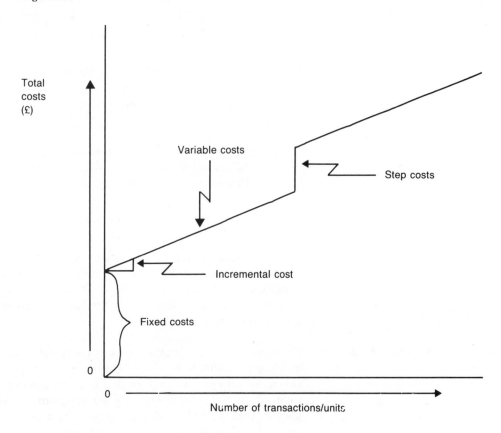

required to perform each transaction (for example staff time, line charges and hit rate charges from the vendor, photocopying of output). The graph shows that incremental costs are equal for each transaction, which is clearly not true for most services. However, for discussion purposes they can be thought of as being linear.

● At some point the volume of services is such that a resource is completely used (for example a terminal is used to its capacity) and more resources must be made or purchased to provide any additional services provided. These costs are referred to as semi-fixed or 'step costs' and must be added to the variable and fixed costs as shown in the figure.

A.2.2.4 Allocation and depreciation of costs

Calculating the total cost of a service would be relatively simple if resources were always dedicated exclusively to specific services. Unfortunately, this is rarely the case except with very large public libraries where, for example, staff can be assigned exclusively to do searching, cataloguing, or interlibrary loans and so on. Even in large public libraries computer equipment and systems are multi-purpose, and facilities are used for most services (except those provided in branch libraries or when older stock is stored in warehousing).

Allocation of costs is the process of determining the extent to which resources are applied to specific services. For example, allocation of staff is done by determining how much time staff spend on specific services and other activities. Examples of methods for allocating staff, stock, equipment and other resources are discussed in Section 6.

A special kind of allocation is done when resources are expensed rather than expended. For example, if equipment is purchased outright, the amount paid is the expenditure. On the other hand, it may well be advantageous to allocate the cost of a resource over the time period it is likely to be used. This allocation process is called depreciation. The amount allocated is an expense. Depreciation involves spreading expenditures for such resources as computer equipment, mobile libraries, vans, facilities and so on.

141

Usually local authorities (or accountants etc) recommend methods of calculation for public libraries. The simplest method of calculating depreciated expenses is to divide expenditures equally among planning years. This can be done using the following steps:

- Establish a useful period of life for the resource; for example, 7 years for a mainframe computer, 5 years for minicomputers, 5 years for mobile libraries and vans, 50 years for buildings etc.

- Estimate a write-off value for the resource at the end of its useful life.

- Subtract the write-off value from the price paid. Calculate the equal annual write-off value: the difference divided by the number of years of useful life.

  For example, for a minicomputer:

$$\frac{£12,000 - £1,200}{5 \text{ years}} = £2,160 \text{ per year}$$

For many reasons, accountants prefer not to use linear depreciation (that is, equal amounts over the years). Reasons are that use of the resource is likely to reduce over time, and that the value of money changes over time. Note that a depreciated cost can, and often is, further allocated among services (in addition to allocation to specific time period).

A.2.2.5 Average or unit costs

Once the fixed and variable costs of resources have been properly allocated, it is possible to calculate total cost over a specified period of time associated with a service or activity. Average or unit costs of services can be calculated by dividing total cost by total output quantity. Examples of average costs include cost per book loaned, cost per online search, cost per item used in library, cost per interlibrary loan etc. This derived performance indicator is extremely useful, but rarely calculated by public libraries. Such averages are probably the single best indicator of how well a library is performing in terms of costs.

The inverse of average cost (that is, quantities produced divided by total cost) is productivity. Average cost is a better indicator than productivity in two ways.

- Productivity is sometimes more difficult to interpret — For example, average cost of online searching could be £50 per search, while the corresponding productivity indicator would be 0.02 searches per pound.

- Average cost, when broken down into components, can be used for budgeting purposes — For example, if a public library has trend data on amount of online searching done, items loaned etc, it is possible to use a forecast of amount of searching to forecast resource requirements as follows:

  — Assume the forecast is 2,000 online searches for a large public library. Further assume average costs are one-half hour of professional staff per search, 10 minutes of support staff per search, 15 minutes of terminal time per search, £15 vendor charges per search, and £1 photocopying costs per search.
  — Resource requirements for the forecast year would be 1,000 hours of professional staff, 333 hours of support staff, 500 hours of terminal time (or approximately a quarter of a terminal), £30,000 for vendor charges, and £2,000 for photocopying. The total forecast cost would be £100,000. Budgeting can be done much more accurately using this method than the traditional method which is to forecast total cost spread over more and more transactions.

Average cost is found by dividing total cost by the number of transactions. One can see in Figure A.1 that average cost decreases as number of transactions increase. For example, assume that the fixed cost of a service, say online searching, is £5,000 and the incremental cost is £50. If there is only one search per year the average cost is £5,050 per search. If there are two searches the average cost is £2,550 (£5,000 + 2 × £50 ÷ 2), three searches £1,716.67, and so on. As the number of searches increases, say to 100 searches, the average cost drops to £150 (£5,000 + 100 × £50

÷ 100), a number much nearer £50, the incremental cost. At 1,000 searches the average cost is £55. We can continue to increase the number of searches and the average cost will continue to come closer to £50 but never quite reach it.

In fact, at some amount of transactions the average cost approaches an 'asymptote' (that is, an amount closely approached but never reached) which, in fact, is the incremental variable cost as shown in Figure A.2. This point at which average cost becomes close to the incremental cost can be thought of as a critical mass. From a public library funder's perspective, it is desirable for services to be provided at or near the critical mass because it is at this point that the difference between costs of services and value received is at its optimum. Public libraries and their branch libraries can achieve a critical mass for such activities as acquisitions and physical processing by centralising the functions to increase number of transactions or units processed.

Figure A.2

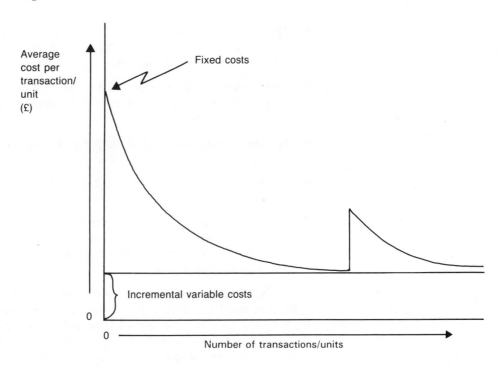

Figure A.2 shows that a 'step cost' will affect average cost, but by less than the entire step cost, because the amount of the step cost is averaged over a large number. For example, assume that a new terminal at £1,000 is required after 1,000 searches (that is, 1,001 searches). The average cost at 1,001 searches then is £55.99 ((£5,000 + £1,000 + 1,001 ÷ £50) ÷ 1,001), a value not much higher than £50, the amount at 1,000 searches without the new terminal. Obviously, a library would not get a terminal to conduct one search, but rather search off-hours etc with the terminal. However, in practice as well as theory, the average cost comes close to that shown in the figure.

Economies of scale can be achieved in other ways as well. For example, large library operations can normally perform some production-like activities less expensively than small ones. An example is processing interlibrary loan requests or cataloguing. By batching these activities, they can normally be done more productively than if they are done in an on-again, off-again manner. Economies of scale can also be achieved in larger library operations by having staff with specialised competencies (that is, knowledge and skills) perform only activities which require their knowledge and skills developed through education, training and experience. The extreme example would be a small library run by a professional librarian who is required to catalogue, search, and open the post.

Finally, large libraries can sometimes obtain volume discounts for purchases of supplies, leases of terminals etc.

There are diseconomies of scale as well. Typically, in public libraries and other organisations it often costs more on the average to administer operations as the size of the organisation increases. That is, *the proportion of total costs accounted for by administration tends to increase as the total costs increase.* There may be many reasons, if and when this happens, but probably the principal reason is that communication and maintaining control is harder in larger organisations.

A.3 Methods for obtaining measured effectiveness and domain indicators

A.3.1 Survey design

There are five basic components of public library surveys:

- Data collection methods — Specific methods for collecting data include observing users in a library, in-person interviews, telephone interviews and self-administered questionnaires.

- Questionnaire design — Each data collection method requires a different type of questionnaire. Each question must be designed to accommodate the specific data collection method.

- Sample design — Aspects of sample design include defining a sampling frame, determining sample size, specific sample design, and selecting a sample.

- Data processing — Data processing can be done by hand tabulation or computer.

- Calculation methods and analysis — There are several types of measured indicators including totals, means (averages), medians and proportions. Each measured and derived indicator may require a specific method of calculation, interpretation and analysis.

These five basic survey components are discussed in detail below.

Keep in mind that a survey is subject to many problems and sources of error. Each survey component is like a link in a chain, where any weak link can damage the validity of the entire survey (regardless of how strong the other components are). Examples are given below to help you avoid some of the most common pitfalls of surveys.

A.3.1.1 Collecting data

There are basically four methods of survey data collection.

Personal interviews

Interviewers ask questions from a survey instrument or interview guide. This method can be used only when it is possible to communicate with respondents directly such as in the library or the respondents' homes or places of work. The interviewers normally ask specific questions and record the answers. They can also clarify the intent or meaning of questions, if asked. Most of the data obtained for measured effectiveness indicators can be precoded and, therefore, recording bias can be kept to a minimum.

Personal interviews have the advantage of permitting complex questions and lengthy interviews. However, neither of these two conditions are necessary for data collection for measured effectiveness indicators. On the other hand, the cost of personal interviews is high because interviewers should be trained and, if the interviews are conducted in homes or workplaces, there are substantial additional costs associated with setting up the interviews, travelling to and from the locations of the interview and calls back when respondents are not available or do not show up.

This survey method should not be used unless:

- the measured effectiveness indicators' data are being collected as part of a larger data collection effort; or

- the data collection is done in the library. (This excludes general population surveys.)

Library staff members can conduct interviews for general user surveys, visitor surveys, or specific service surveys. The interviewers should be those who are not associated with any specific service for which data are being collected (for example report response times, satisfaction with quality, timeliness, availability, access, for specific services).

Telephone interviews

Telephone interviews can be used for general population surveys to reduce high costs associated with personal interviews in homes or workplaces. However, there are some drawbacks with telephone interviews:

- listings of telephone numbers exclude persons who do not have telephones and do not include ex-directory numbers;

- telephone interviews require a greater degree of structure (although this may not be required for data for most measured effectiveness indicators);

- telephone interviews are generally briefer than personal interviews, because it is more difficult to retain attention.

However, the telephone interview is an excellent means for conducting surveys, if staff or volunteers can be freed to conduct the interviews and enough telephones are available. This method has the distinct advantage over self-administered questionnaires (see below) in that one can expect higher response rates (that is, number of completed questionnaires divided by number of persons sampled). This method is more costly than self-administered questionnaires however.

Self-administered questionnaires

Another common data collection method is to mail or hand out questionnaires to individuals who fill them out and return them to the library. This method is inexpensive and has the advantage of letting respondents fill out the questionnaires at their own pace and to think about their responses more thoroughly. However, this method has the distinct disadvantage of low response rates. Typical postal questionnaires, for example, often result in less than 20% responses, and question-naires handed out in libraries often result in less than one-third responses.

Those who voluntarily complete a questionnaire may be different from those who do not (for example they may be frequent users, less busy, more literate). Generally, one should aim for more than 50% response rates. From a cost standpoint it is far better to have a smaller initial sample and achieve higher response rates (through telephone interviews, telephone follow-ups to non-respondents or some other means of follow-up) than to have a large sample with low response rates.

Observation of users in a library

One can observe users in the library to determine what services and resources they use. If the observations can be made unobtrusively, one can measure extent of use of the services and resources. On the other hand, the method is very limited in the number of measures that can be obtained and must be accompanied by collecting data (from the same persons) on frequency of visits and use, satisfaction and so on.

If all the information that is collected is for measured and derived indicators, a combination of telephone interviews and self-administered questionnaires will suf-fice. For example, when visitors leave the library they can be asked to fill out a questionnaire at that time (with tables or desks set aside to do this) or asked to fill it out at home and return it (on a subsequent visit or by post – a stamped addressed envelope can help). The sampled person can be asked for name and telephone number to permit telephone follow-up (to clarify responses if necessary) or to obtain the information over the telephone if the person has not responded.

Questionnaire design for all four types of surveys is a critical element in the chain of events leading to valid and reliable indicators. Most surveys require a data collection instrument or questionnaire. Therefore, procedures should be followed to ensure that correct answers to questions are obtained and errors are not made. Ideally, questionnaires should be pretested by personal or telephone interview, if possible, to discover respondents' understanding of the questions and the instructions given. In addition, the pretests provide an assessment of the duration of the interview or time necessary for respondents. Also, pretests of self-administered questionnaires provide a means for assessing the response rates that can be expected.

In designing survey questionnaires, four basic rules should be kept in mind:

- Ask only for the minimum information required.

- Make sure that the questions *can* be answered.

- Make sure that the questions can be answered *truthfully*.

- Make sure that the questions *will* be answered.

To guarantee these basics, the rules below should be followed in phrasing questions and in formatting a questionnaire:

1. *Verbiage* — Questions should be phrased using the smallest number of words, everyday words, and words that are unambiguous and make sense. This especially applies to self-administered questionnaires, since some respondents will skip a long preamble to a question and go straight on to answer the question regardless of ambiguities.

2. *Complex questions* — Two or more questions should not be disguised under one question expecting a simple answer. For example, one should avoid questions like, 'On your last visit to the library did you conduct bibliographic searches using published bibliographies or online searching? -- YES/NO.' That is three questions in one, and unless three response boxes are set up, answers will be meaningless.

3. *Complex/inverted questions* — Questions should be phrased so that if the respondent agrees with the statement he or she can answer 'Yes' (that is, do not use negatives in such a way as to invert the question).

4. *Recall* — It is difficult for respondents to remember events over, say, one month. The way to avoid this problem is to rely on critical incidents, such as 'When did you last conduct an online search?' or 'How many online searches did you conduct last month?' These questions are more likely to give reliable answers than 'How many times did you conduct online searches last year?'

5. *Concrete facts versus opinions* — Answers to questions about what people actually do are likely to be more reliable than answers to questions about what they like, feel, or want for the future. For example, questions about future purchase behaviour or price that respondents will pay for an information product or service are not very reliable.

6. Use *'critical incidents'* of use of services when possible rather than general statements. For example 'What was your level of satisfaction with the response time of your last online search?' is preferable to 'What is your level of satisfaction with online searches?'

7. *Keep the questionnaire short* — It is important that a question be included only if it is essential. Lengthy questionnaires, which the respondent may not see the need for, tend to result in thoughtless answers and lower response rates.

8. *Make sure the first few questions are particularly important ones* whose relevance can be seen by the respondent. Extra care should be taken with the substance and phrasing of these first few questions. In order to avoid conditioning answers to subsequent questions by what is asked in earlier ones, it is best to go from general questions to specific questions and go from the simple to the difficult questions.

9. *Place open-ended questions near the end of the questionnaire* so that the closed questions will be answered before the respondent tires. Boring or repetitive questions especially should be placed at the end of a questionnaire to avoid respondent refusal. The objective of organising the questionnaire is to provide a sequence that is natural and easy for the respondent; therefore, topics and questions need to be arranged in the pattern which makes the most sense to the respondent.

Above all, when designing questionnaires it is important for the questionnaire designer to visualise how easily the respondent can answer each question.

One of the biggest problems with surveys is refusal to respond, particularly with self-administered questionnaires. Ways to avoid non-response are to make sure self-administered questionnaires are brief, have good typographic quality, and deal with interesting issues. Respondents are unable to understand the relevance of a survey when there are inadequate explanations, badly worded questions and poorly ordered questions. Personal questions will achieve lower response rates and may contribute to respondents' refusal of the whole questionnaire. Questions that are not understood by respondents will be refused. Finally, questions concerning attitudes may achieve lower response rates than more straightforward factual questions.

Almost every survey will require that results be classified into certain groups, so that one can see, for example, how women's behaviour differs from that of men, or how school-aged children use library services, or how level of education affects use of libraries. The demographic characteristics to include depend on the type of survey being conducted and which characteristics might be related to differences in behaviour.

A.3.2 Statistical sample design

Statistical sampling methods are used for three purposes. They:

- provide a formal mechanism for making sure that we obtain the most precise estimate possible for a given budget;

- help ensure that correct (unbiased and accurate) estimates are obtained;

- provide a formal means of estimating the precision of the observations made.

Inherent in the statistical methods are procedures for determining what sample sizes are necessary for achieving certain levels of statistical precision. This section discusses statistical estimates, procedures, sampling methods, and sample designs.

There are four important aspects of sample design.

- *Sampling frame* — It is necessary to form a sampling frame of the objects or people from which a sample will be chosen. The objects may be people, households or telephone listings in the community for a general population survey, registered users for a general user survey, library visitors for visitor surveys, and lists of users for specific services surveys.

- *Sample design* — There are a number of sampling designs that can be used to improve the survey precision and/or cost effectiveness.

- *Sample size* — The number of persons chosen for the sample depends on required precision of estimates of totals, averages, proportions etc.

- *Sample selection* — After a sampling frame is developed, sample design established, and sample size determined, a method for randomly choosing respondents can be selected.

Aspects of sample design are discussed below.

Sampling frame

It is best to assemble a list of all people or other units (for example time-slots) that are going to be sampled. This list is referred to as the sampling frame. Generally, for visitor surveys, you should choose periods of time and then select visitors who come to the library during that period.

To begin with it is important, if possible, to know the total number of people (or households) in the population being surveyed and assemble a list of these. We can then gauge the probability that individuals will be sampled. For general population surveys the population of residents may be obtained from local authorities. However, developing a list may be very difficult. Market researchers would assemble lists of households and draw samples (actually clusters) of households to visit and interview. This kind of household personal interview survey is prohibitively expensive for most library surveys.

A better sampling frame is a telephone listing. As mentioned earlier, problems with this list are its currency, households that do not have telephones, and households that do not list their numbers in the directory. The first and third problems can be addressed by random digit dialling. That is, for a portion of the survey one can choose random number and dial them to obtain at least some responses from unlisted households. (One must establish whether or not the household that answers has a listed numbers and, if so, include the survey response as part of that portion of the survey.) Once the household is reached it is necessary to determine how many persons there are in the household and either have the person who answers the telephone respond or randomly select (that is, rotate) among the type of respondents desired, for example male adult, female adult or child.

For households that do not have listed telephone numbers, it may suffice to do a small household personal interview in areas or neighbourhoods where it is known that it is less likely that there are telephones. However, it is difficult to do household interviews in these areas and an alternative is to go to local grocery shops and ask customers if they have a telephone and, if not, do the interview with them. Usually 25 such interviews are sufficient. This form of sampling is not statistically desirable, but it is practical.

Lists of the daytime population are even more difficult to obtain because many of these people work in the library service area but do not live there. The way to sample this population is to sample businesses and government agencies and then choose up to five persons from each organisation in a random-like manner (for example from a company or agency phone listing). Again, usually about 25 to 50 persons from this population will suffice.

A list of registered borrowers can serve as the sampling frame for general user surveys. Sometimes such lists contain names of people who are no longer residents. So, when the survey is being conducted it is important to keep track of the number of registered borrowers who no longer have valid membership. Probably the best design for this survey is to contact the sampled registered borrowers by telephone.

For users of special services (for example outreach, reference) it is best to choose a list of relatively recent users, such as those who have used the service within the last one to three months (depending on relative frequency of use). If a list is not normally available from logs or other records, it is useful to assemble a list prior to the survey. It is important that the list of names be unique (that is, each name appears only once) and not merely a reflection of amount of use; otherwise frequent users will have a higher probability of selection.

Sample design

Simple random sampling is the most basic statistical design, although, for several reasons that are discussed below, it is rarely used. As the name implies, the design is based on random sampling from a list (sample frame) of individuals. The basis of the random sample is to be able to assign a probability of selection to each item or unit in the sample frame. A simple random sample implies that each unit has an equal chance of selection. For this to be true, it is necessary to construct a sampling frame and establish a selection procedure.

- Define the population to be sampled. A population might be telephone listings, number of registered borrowers, number of users of specific services etc.

- Identify all specific units within the population so that they can have a known chance to be chosen in a sample. The identity of units, which are frequently listed, is called a sample frame, and the items on the list are called sample units.

- Assign a sequential number to the items on the list.

- Choose individual sample units (or numbers) – the sample selection procedure. Some statisticians insist that the sample be chosen in a completely random manner, using tables of random numbers. To do this each random number is chosen and then looked up on the sample frame.

  This process is quite time-consuming. However, a perfectly valid method, which is far more practical, is to use a systematic sample with random start, thus:

  — take the desired sample size and divide that number into the number of sample units in the sample frame;

  — sample through the list using that interval (called the sampling interval). Suppose we have a list of 2,000 registered borrowers. If 200 interviews are desired, divide 2,000 by 200 to establish a sampling interval of 10. Next, draw a random number between 1 and 10 to use as a starting point in the sample – say 7. With a sampling interval of 10, the sampled units would be the 7th and every 10th borrower beyond that (that is, 17, 27, 37, . . .).

The only caveat about using a systematic sample with random start is that there can be periodicity in a listing which can bias the sample selection. For example, suppose the sample frame is a list of days over-time. A sample interval of seven would mean that a specific day would always be chosen. This means that differences among days would not be taken into account in the sample procedure described. One should make a judgement about possible periodicity prior to using a systematic sample with random start.

There are statistical sample methods that are designed to provide better results than the simple random sample. One of these designs, stratified random sampling, takes advantage of information known about the sampling units in order to provide more statistically precise estimates. For example, if we know that adults use libraries more than children, the sample designer can apply this information to improve the sample design. In effect, sample estimates can be made more precise by taking into account the differences between strata. The precision is determined by well-known statistical equations.

Three criteria should be kept in mind for allocating the sample size to the strata (for example adults *versus* children or age groups). In a given stratum it is usually best to take a larger sample if any of the following conditions is true:

- the stratum is larger than the others;

- the stratum is more variable;

- the sampling is less expensive to conduct in the stratum.

In the absence of appropriate information about the strata, one will not go too far wrong by using the same sample fraction in each stratum.

In making population estimates from stratified random samples it is important to take into account the disproportionate sampling among strata.

Another statistical sample design involves the situation in which the sample units of interest are part of a larger unit. For example, the survey may involve online search users, who would be associated with branch libraries that do online searching. Here one may want to determine time spent searching, satisfaction with search results, or other information. If the number of users or online searches is large, a subsample of them is taken. This procedure is called two-stage sampling: the primary sampling units in the example are branch libraries, and the online searches by users are the secondary sampling units. That is, one first chooses a sample of branch libraries, then a sample of online searches from each of the sampled branch libraries. Sometimes the primary units are referred to as clusters if the number of secondary units is not identified or known before the sample is drawn.

Another statistical method that has proved extremely useful in improving the precision of estimates is ratio estimation. This method uses an auxiliary variable about which one has information in order to calibrate estimates. In this method it is assumed that the auxiliary variable is highly correlated to the variable of interest. For example, the amount of interlibrary lending performed in a library is probably highly correlated to the size of a library, as measured, for example, by holdings. If one knows the number of holdings but not number of interlibrary loans, the holdings can be used as an auxiliary variable.

Sample size

Sample size determines in part the precision of estimates made from sample surveys. What level of precision is necessary depends on the consequences of making a wrong decision or otherwise misinterpreting survey results. Sometimes precise estimates are crucial – for example when testing drugs from a production line. Effectiveness indicators do not have to be very precise.

Generally, sample sizes for the four types of surveys should be of the following order of magnitude:

- General population survey: 250–400 respondents.

- General user survey: 150–300 respondents.

- Visitor survey: 150–300 respondents.

- Specific service user survey: 100–250 respondents.

There is a tendency to over-sample rather than under-sample. Below are some statistical concepts that need to be understood concerning precision of estimates and effect of sample size on precision.

The precision of estimates is commonly represented by confidence intervals. For example, suppose we had a simple random sample size of 200 library visitors. We estimated that 0.50 (or 50%) of our sample was female. We could display the confidence interval as:

50% ± 3.5%; at 68% level of confidence.

Simply said, this means that we can be 68% certain that between 46.5% and 53.5% of our entire visitor population was female.

We can easily determine confidence intervals for any desired level of confidence by multiplying the confidence interval (that is, 3.5% above) by a constant factor. For example, to estimate the confidence interval at 95% level of confidence, we need merely to multiply the confidence interval by the factor 1.96. The confidence interval above would then be expressed as:

50% ± 6.9%; at 95% level of confidence.

The factor for estimating 90% levels of confidence is 1.64, and it is 3.00 for estimating 99.8% levels of confidence.

The width of confidence intervals (at a specified level of confidence) depends on four factors. So these four factors affect how sure we can be of the validity of our results:

1. *Sample size* — For example, the estimates above are estimated from a sample size of 200 observations. If we doubled the sample size to 400, the confidence interval would decrease from 3.5% to 2.5% at 68% level of confidence. If the sample were reduced to 100, the confidence interval would increase from 3.5% to 5.0% at 68% level of confidence. *The larger the sample, the more reliable the results*.

2. *Sample size relative to population size* — If the sample size were in fact the entire population, the confidence interval would be zero. All our examples assume that the sample size is very small compared with the population size. Since the sample size of some types of library users may be reasonably high compared with the population of users, there is some gain in reduced confidence intervals. For the example above, if one assumes that a sample of 100 users of a service is from a population of 300 users the confidence interval would fall from 5.0% to 4.1%.

3. *Inherent variability of observations* — For example if specified levels of importance of interlibrary lending and reference services ranged from 1 to 5, the confidence interval for the estimated average level of performance would probably be greater than estimates in which levels ranged from 3 to 5.

4. *Sample design* — A survey can be improved in terms of decreasing estimated confidence levels (at a given sample size) by statistical sample design (for example stratification, ratio estimation).

Examples of standard error (at 68% level of confidence) for various sample sizes and estimated proportions (%) are given in Table A.1.

Table A.1

Sample size	Estimated proportion (%)					
	5–95%	10–90%	20–80%	30–70%	40–60%	50%
25	4.3	6.0	8.0	9.2	9.8	10.0
50	3.1	4.2	5.7	6.5	6.9	7.1
75	2.5	3.5	4.6	5.3	5.7	5.8
100	2.2	3.0	4.0	4.6	4.9	5.0
150	1.8	2.4	3.3	3.7	4.0	4.1
200	1.5	2.1	2.8	3.2	3.5	3.5
250	1.4	1.9	2.5	3.0	3.1	3.2
400	1.1	1.5	2.0	2.3	2.4	2.5

Note that complementary proportions (95% for 5%, 70% for 30% etc) have exactly the same standard errors.

This table can be used to determine sample sizes initially or to test approximate statistical precision of survey results. For example, if we expect about 30% of users to have borrowed books on their last visit as we are willing to accept estimates between about 25% and 35% at 68% level of confidence, a sample size of about 85 is sufficient. Note, however, that this means 85 completed responses (not the number of questionnaires handed out or posted). Assume that a sample of 152 responses was received and the proportion of users who used the card catalogue was estimated to be 10%. The confidence level for this estimate would be about 2.4% at the 68% level of confidence or 4.7% at the 95% level of confidence (2.4 × 1.96 = 4.7).

It is useful to note that if certain stratum results are particularly important the sample size of that stratum should partially determine sample size. For example, if it is important to know results for children (or adults), the sample size for children (or adults) should be considered and the table above used as a guide for how many children to sample.

Remember, however, that there can be sources of bias in survey results. For example, respondents must recall number of visits in the last month or aspects of the most recent item borrowed etc. Such reported data are unlikely to be exact. The data, however, are likely to be in the right order of magnitude since respondents have a sense for how they handle such incidents. One can also attempt to minimise the problem of recall by using critical incidents of borrowing, use of reference services etc.

Appendix B.   Glossary of terms

ALLOCATED COSTS — Costs that have been divided among the services on which they were incurred. For example, the division of terminal or computer costs among cataloguing, interlibrary borrowing, and online bibliographic searching.

ATTRIBUTE — An inherent characteristic of a resource, service or product, use, user etc. For example, attributes of staff include competence, experience etc; attributes of library services include quality, timeliness, availability, accessibility etc; attributes of use include purpose of use; attributes of users include information need, age, occupation etc.

AVERAGE OR UNIT COST — The financial resources needed to provide one unit of service.

COST — Cost usually associated with the amount of resources or services applied (or devoted) to activities, services etc. For example, using staff to perform an activity incurs the costs of staff time applied to the activity. The amount of resource can be converted to funds. Since funds or money is a financial resource, an expenditure is the application of the funds or money for purchasing (or employing) resources.

COST AND BENEFITS — The cost (that is, detriments) and benefits of a library service are the unfavourable and favourable comparisons of a service and the alternatives to the service in terms of differences in input, output, performance and effectiveness. For example, the value added by a given service, over that of an alternative to the service, could consist of a lower cost and/or a superior performance. The alternatives to the service might consist of the clients performing the work themselves or engaging a consultant or outside company to perform the work.

COST FINDING — A less formal method than cost accounting to determine costs, using available financial data and recasting and adjusting it to derive the cost data needed.

DEPRECIATION — A method of allocating the cost of an asset to the particular time period for which cost analysis is performed.

DIRECT COSTS — Costs that are readily attributable to a specific service, resource, or activity.

ECONOMIES OF SCALE — Situation in which average (or unit) costs decrease for increasing number of transactions or units of services.

EFFECTIVENESS — Effectiveness is measured from the perspective of clients or users of library services. Examples of measures of effectiveness include user satisfaction with a service, repeated use of a service and number of times a service is used (first order effects). Higher order effects would include effect of services on the user's research and consequences of the user's research, improved productivity of the user's operation or research etc. Presumably, improved quality, timeliness, availability etc should result in greater user satisfaction and increased use. Thus, library service output performance partially determines the effectiveness of the service.

EFFICIENCY — Efficiency is an indicator of how closely an activity approaches maximum or optimum values. For example, public library staff rarely work all of their time on specific operational activities. There is some time wasted due to shifting from one activity to another, tea breaks, talking to colleagues, thinking about non-work related things and so on. Typically, work efficiency is in the order of magnitude of about 65%, although generally small libraries tend to be less efficient than large libraries. Efficiency is computed by dividing amount actually worked, used etc by the amount possible. Efficiency is not to be confused with productivity which is the ratio of output quantities divided by amount of time or cost (see definition of productivity below). An operation or activity can be inefficient but productive and vice versa. Productivity is probably the more useful indicator of the two, but efficiency should be calculated because it may be found that productivity is low because staff, equipment use, or facility use etc is inefficient.

EXPENDITURE — Expenditure is the amount of funds paid for resources or services at the time money is exchanged or owed. It is the cost of acquiring resources or services. Expenditure is not to be confused with expense, which is a calculation of the cost incurred when the resource or service is used. (See definition of expense, below.) For example, a microcomputer may be purchased in one year but used for five years. The purchase of the computer is an expenditure. Subdividing the cost (for example equally) over the years calculates the expense or annual cost. Expenditure and expense should be the same if the resource or service is consumed or used over a short period of time.

EXPENSE — Expense is a calculation or estimate of the amount paid for a resource or service when it is used (not to be confused with expenditure – see above). The process of calculating expense of a resource is referred to as depreciation. A resource or service is depreciated over specified periods of time (for example each of five years in the future).

FACTORS THAT AFFECT LIBRARY SERVICE INPUT, OUTPUT, PERFORMANCE AND EFFECTIVENESS

- Factors that affect input might include staff characteristics, equipment attributes etc;

- Factors that might affect output or performance (in addition to amount of input resources) are management (policies, capabilities, attitudes etc), physical environment, attitude or capability of users etc;

- Factors that might affect effectiveness (in addition to output performance) are user awareness of, attitudes toward, or perception of a library service, a charge for the service, distance to the service, communication constraints etc.

Some factors are internal and therefore controllable. Other factors are external and less controllable by library management.

FIXED COSTS — Costs that remain constant regardless of changes in the activity level or method of providing the activity.

FULLY ALLOCATED ACTIVITY COST — The total cost of an activity, including both direct and indirect costs.

FULL-TIME EQUIVALENT — A measure of the total workforce in which the hours worked by part-time employees are summed together and counted as if they applied to full-time staff. Thus, a staff of 12 full-time employees and 3 half-time employees would total 13.5 full time equivalents, commonly abbreviated as FTE.

FUNCTIONAL POPULATION ATTRACTORS — These are the facilities and operations within a locality which may encourage people to go to live in the area.

INCREMENTAL COSTS — The amount of variable costs associated with each transaction or unit.

INDICATORS — Sometimes it is not possible to measure input, output, performance or effectiveness directly. Thus, indicators must suffice. Indicators of a librarian's competence are degrees held, university attended, professional awards given, elected position in a professional society etc. Indicators may be needed for higher order effects. For example, an indicator of research output is number of laboratory notes or articles written which report the research.

INDIRECT COSTS — Costs that are not easily assignable or really attributable to any one service, activity, or function.

- Indirect operating costs — These costs include centrally budgeted items (for example utilities, rent, insurance, etc) that are necessary to the general operation and maintenance of the library system.

- Indirect support costs — Costs for support services that benefit overall administration of the library system and its services (for example administration, accounting, personnel, etc).

INPUT — There are several input resources necessary to offer/perform services. These input resources include capital, staff, equipment, facilities, information, supplies, administrative and support staff etc. Each resource component can be measured in several ways; for example, staff can be measured in Full-Time Equivalents, number of persons, hours of work, or cost (salary, on-costs, overhead).

LINKAGE OF PUBLIC LIBRARY SERVICES' INPUT TO OUTPUT, AND LIBRARY SERVICE PERFORMANCE TO EFFECTIVENESS — Linkage is correlation and/or mathematical models which show that:

- output performance depends on input resources in addition to other factors;

- first order effects (for example frequency of use of a service) depend on output performance in addition to other factors;

- higher order effects depend on first order effects.

Examples of such analysis and models include correlation and multiple regression, conjoint measurement, factor analysis, multi-aggregate regression etc.

MEASURE — In the context of this manual, measure is often used generally to mean any process for describing in quantitative values things, people, events etc. In a true sense we would normally measure distances such as shelving, count people on staff or visits to a library, record duration of time such as responding to requests for online searches, observe what users or staff are doing such as studying at tables or shelving stock, survey users or staff behaviour, satisfaction with services etc, compute costs, and so on. Measure can either be the process of description (that is, counting, recording etc) or the result of the process (that is, number of staff, time in days etc).

ON-COST — This is the additional cost of staff, over and above the actual salary, pension and insurance payments made on their behalf – the cost of training, time off-the-job etc.

OUTPUT — Measures of output of library services include quantities of output (for example number of items acquired, number of items circulated, number of searches performed), quality of service, timeliness of services provided, availability and accessibility of library staff and facilities etc.

PERFORMANCE — Performance is an indication of how well a service or activity is performed. It can be measured in terms of the output quantities produced, quality, timeliness, availability, accessibility etc. Other indications of performance are productivity, efficiency (that is, how close services or activities come to achieving some maximum) etc. Output performance determines the effectiveness of services (see below). Measures of productivity, efficiency etc are measures which are internal to the service and they are used to help manage an operation such as the library.

PRODUCTIVITY — Productivity is measured as output divided by input. It relates the quantity of goods and services produced (output) and the quantity of labour, capital, land, energy and other resources that produced it (input). Productivity is a measure which links input and output. The weakness of the traditional measure of productivity is that there is an interdependence among amount of input resources, output quantities produced, and other output measures such as quality, timeliness etc. For example, a librarian's competence will affect both input (amount of time and cost necessary to perform a service) as well as output (amount, quality and timeliness of service).

SEMI-FIXED COSTS ('STEP COSTS') — Costs that are fixed at a certain level of activity, but change with large increases or decreases in activity level.

SERVICE — Library services may be defined at several levels. Examples of types of services include:

- technical services such as cataloguing etc;

- user-related services such as reference or access to a collection;

- services provided by administrators. Such library services can be subdivided into discrete activities necessary to perform them (for example contacting a user, negotiating what is needed, performing online searches, reporting results).

Each activity may require several resource components (for example staff, equipment).

VARIABLE COSTS — Costs that change directly with changes in the level of activity or method of performing the activity. Examples are:

- *Staff salaries* — Includes only staff time associated with providing a service or producing a product.

- *Other variable* — Includes all other costs associated with providing a service or producing a product.

Appendix C.   Performance Indicators Advisory Committee

Chairman	C C Leamy	Office of Arts and Libraries
Secretaries	D Ferris/M Smith	British Library Research and Development Department
Panel	P Beauchamp	Office of Arts and Libraries
	S Brewer	Chief Librarian Newcastle upon Tyne Public Libraries
	R Craig	Scottish Library Association
	M Grieves	Research Development Department British Library
	D Jones	Richmond upon Thames Public Libraries
	J Jones	County Library Hertfordshire County Council
	D Leabeater	National Consumer Council
	M Redfern	Library Association
Consultants	Don King/ J-M Griffiths	King Research Ltd

Printed in the United Kingdom for HMSO
Dd 292996   C16   9/90